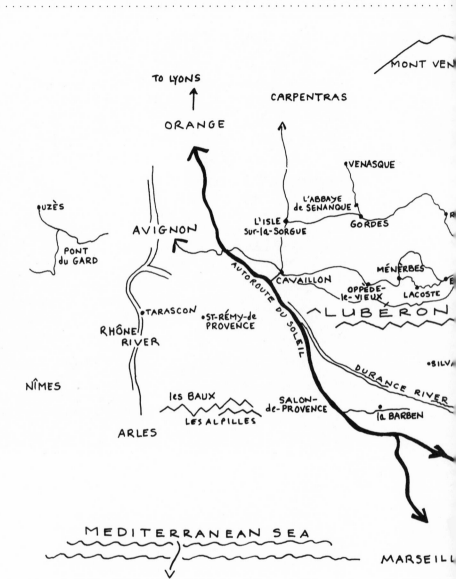

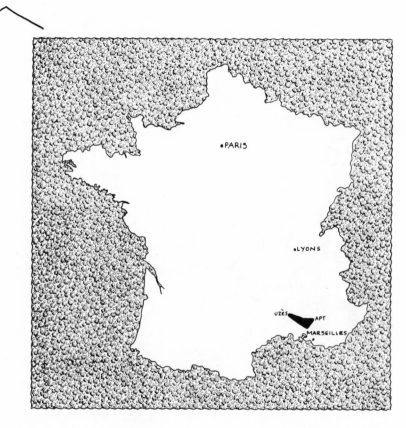

APT

•PARIS

•LYONS

UZÈS APT
MARSEILLES

X-EN-
ROVENCE

TO CANNES →
and NICE

A WINDOW ON PROVENCE

*One Summer's Sojourn
into the Simple Life*

BO NILES

PENGUIN BOOKS

PENGUIN BOOKS
Published by the Penguin Group
Viking Penguin, a division of Penguin Books USA Inc.,
375 Hudson Street, New York, New York 10014, U.S.A.
Penguin Books Ltd, 27 Wrights Lane, London W8 5TZ, England
Penguin Books Australia Ltd, Ringwood, Victoria, Australia
Penguin Books Canada Ltd, 2801 John Street,
Markham, Ontario, Canada L3R 1B4
Penguin Books (N.Z.) Ltd, 182–190 Wairau Road,
Auckland 10, New Zealand

Penguin Books Ltd, Registered Offices:
Harmondsworth, Middlesex, England

First published in the United States of America
by Viking Penguin, a division of Penguin Books USA Inc., 1990
Published in Penguin Books 1991

1   3   5   7   9   10   8   6   4   2

Line drawings by the author

Grateful acknowledgment is made to Lizzie Napoli and her publisher Rivages
for permission to reprint a tone poem and a recipe for pistou
from *Carnets de Voyage en Provence*. © Rivages, 1987.

THE LIBRARY OF CONGRESS HAS CATALOGUED THE HARDCOVER AS FOLLOWS:
Niles, Bo.
A window on Provence : one summer's sojourn into the simple life / Bo Niles.
p.   cm.
ISBN 0-670-82722-3 (hc.)
ISBN 0 14 01.2022 X (pbk.)
1. Provence (France)—Social life and customs.   2. Country living—
France—Provence.   I. Title.
DC611.P961N55   1990
944'.9—dc20   89–40699

Printed in the United States of America

To Michael

A WINDOW ON PROVENCE

8 *July*

The Train à Grande Vitesse departs precisely *à l'heure,* on time, always and to the minute, at 10:30 A.M. Her needle-nosed engine shrugs, bristles, then shimmies nervously along the railway platform under the glass canopy of the station onto the railway track. Reined in like the thoroughbred she is, the TGV strains for release from the iron tether of the *gare.* Unleashed, she attains a flat-out speed of 120 mph; she can make Avignon in under four hours.

Sliding out of the station and past the dour housing slabs that girdle center-city Paris in a stranglehold of anonymous gloom, the TGV tensed today for speed, shifting gears, and then slammed into full throttle. Like arching off a highboard into the shock of a deep, cool pool, I jolted too, out of the buzz of New York City overload. The impact of sabbatical hit. I would be here for a full month.

But I couldn't quite shake residual tensions, and a feeling of being up-in-the-air, still, airplane-buzzy, not yet grounded. Even the company of a good friend in Paris, coaxing me out of the cocoon of transatlantic flight with good conversation, good wine, a good bed, couldn't quell transition jitters. Suspension. Feeling somewhere between "there" and "here." This feeling is difficult for me to shrug off on any vacation, and again stubbornly persisted—even though this is the third sojourn in Provence, and in the same house, too.

Because Paris is a city, being there for a day or two usually eases the transition from New York; being there extends the way I live and think and act back home, and whenever I arrive, I find I—consciously and unconsciously—sustain the observant mode of the design editor and writer I am. I always begin my Parisian interludes by taking a tour to stake a claim to her architectural treasures.

And so it was this time, too, running off to catch I. M. Pei's shimmering Pyramide in front of the Louvre, judging it, still as editor, not merely as tourist, nor as visitor. I liked it: a translucent handkerchief parachuted over the vast open square, frozen there by the grace of Pei's icy wand. I like its tidy geometry, its grid, the way its taut and tender skin gleams against the Louvre's grandiloquent stone. And I stampeded the new Musée d'Orsay too, brain buzzing from lack of sleep, to see the sweet, damp, and limpid Parisian light pouring in through its crystalline ceiling scrim to fill the great open central nave of the museum as if it were a glorious chalice. But why weren't the Impressionist paintings, removed to this museum from the Jeu de Paume, granted this dearest light? Hanging instead along mean-spirited upper-story galleries, the canvases appeared sapped of their tender energy, crowded, each masterpiece somehow diminished in the crush of the ensemble.

Zoop. The TGV's speed, an extravagance of velocity, whipped the windows of the train hurling Paris backward in its thunderous wake. I couldn't focus on the land seething by outside. It had been cold in Paris as usual, and shrouded in mist and fog, as usual, and every image there had been imprinted on my eye like blown-out grainy film, or old movie stills constricted in monochrome. I felt, in fact, monochromatic still, like a Dorothy whisking on the tail of a great gray tornado through a great gray sky over gray land. When would vacation ensnare me, and, like Oz, disclose itself—color-enhanced and saturated with sensation?

As the train pushed into the heart of France, into the countryside near Burgundy on its approach to Lyons and the Midi, vistas began to fast-forward against the windows. Fields, dense with wheat, pulsated in and out of sight. Because June rains bathed all of France, the land—from the outskirts of Paris and straight on through—looked swollen and almost unbearably fecund. Just four years ago, when I rode this route in reverse in late August with Bill and David and Peter after our first summer trip as a family to visit with my parents in Provence, these same fields had been cauterized, burned black for acres and acres, so that they could regenerate themselves from the nourishment of ash.

Settling into the thudding song of wheel-speed, I recalled that vacation—and a reprise two years later—when we made this house I raced towards on this train our home base. We toured and explored, we tested our mettle as a family of travelers—we had a wonderful time. We gave ourselves two short guidebook vacations; we were frankly tourists then, hitting the "hotspots" from Arles to Avignon to Apt. We tried to see everything within the circle of our vacation valley, and even some sites just beyond. David, a budding teenager, loved the Roman coliseum in Arles and the stories of gladiators who fought there, and Peter, six and a half years younger, cheered Renaults and Peugeots across the taut arches of the Pont du Gard.

This time I've come alone. Bill's workload precluded any extended time off and David chose to take a hike-and-bike adventure trip and Peter is settled into a camp in Maine. This time: It would be just me—and my parents. They have already spent six summers here, initially visiting for a short spell, and then renting from a British friend in two-to-three-month spurts. My father, a composer, utilizes his summer, free-time, away from managing the orchestra he founded in New York, to fulfill any annual musical commissions, and my mother paints and reads and generally protects Dad's self-imposed solitude. I will read here, too, and make collages, I hope, and write within this gift of time and place. But I have to ask: How will it feel to be apart from my grown-up family, the family I've created through marriage and motherhood, and how will it feel besides to be thrown back into the child-family I left a quarter century ago? How will it feel to be just a daughter again, alone with my parents and without my husband and children to define me? And what is it about this particular house, this particular place, this summer, this interlude that I crave?

Zoop. Another TGV whooshed by. The thud of compressed motion, train against passing train, created a sensation like hands clapping.

Or an abrupt gasp for breath.

I gasped, too, with the train. I must find my breath, my rhythm, my balance. Yesterday, in Paris, trailing Deborah as she made her market rounds for dinner provisions, I struggled with rhythm, out of sync with the calmer pace I would assume in Provence, like a recording bouncing from one rpm to another until the soundtrack becomes clear.

Part of this, I guess, was simply culture shock, part of it jet lag, and part of it defenses I carry around like a cloak back home. Blunting my senses in New York, I swaddle them against the pain of squalor, of homelessness, of pollution and noise. I muffle my ears and eyes to the fire lane, hospital emergency access, traffic, car alarms, and occasional gunshots that punctuate my neighborhood. At the airport, I told Deborah, I had been scooped up by a taxi driver jumping the queue who had herded me and my suitcase into his cab. Expecting insolence, I was startled by his explaining that he wanted to compose himself, to grace his 7:30 A.M. sunrise-tinged rearview window with the *visage d'une belle femme*—pretty face—and not with the sulking countenance of a hurried, harried international businessman! Relax, Deborah laughed: You are not in New York.

Arrival: Aswarm with embarking and debarking passengers, the Avignon station stunned me after the lull of a nap on the train, plunged me back into stupor, tossing me into momentary panic. Where were my parents? I suppose I trusted a childlike instinct, like some dowsing rod, to guide me, spontaneously, to them. I stalled, let the crowds thin. And then: There they were, Moth (short for Mother, and because she collects and paints butterflies) and Dad. They stood, quietly, as if arrested in freeze-frame inside a video blur. They'd seen me first, and, catching my glance, now waved, side by side, arm in arm, in matching navy blue polo shirts. I should have known! When my two sisters and I were young, Moth always dressed us alike so that she could find the three-sisters-as-one in a crowd. Ha!

Even so, and perhaps because of that, I remained rooted; I could not move towards them. I could see, right away, that, even though they had preceded me here by only three days, they had already assumed that placid, slightly smug demeanor that comes from feeling perfectly settled. Because they come to this place and this house every summer, our landlord, Michael, who rents his hospitable vacation retreat as a friend to his friends, lets them lock away their chummy belongings after each stay. And so—*pop*—out come the family photographs, the Big Band tapes, the breakfast trays, the sauté pan—and they are at home. I have come with only one suitcase; would I settle in as quickly? I learned Dad's travel lesson implanted in my sisters and me perhaps too well: If you cannot carry it in one hand, leave it behind. As a student, I'd whittled my bag to practically nothing: toothbrush, change of shifts, underwear, sandals. This summer I am not so spartan as that, but I've packed light.

—How is the house?

—All set! [I knew it]

—And the car?

—It's a Mouse, a "Souris."

And so it was, a brand-new, buy-now-and-return-later Renault, a fat four-door gray Mouse. Moth always confers a name on her vehicle of the moment, oftentimes a vegetable, or the occasional fruit: the Zucchini; the Pomodoro, an Italian tomato; the Cerise, a cherry. The thought of a gray food disgusted her, so we would ride in a Mouse this summer.

We fit easily into the accommodating Souris, and within moments were on the road. In the excitement of finally being here, I did not even mind the environs of Avignon, the boxy compounds that solder themselves, barnacle-like, to every old town, or the strip *shopping,* or the gas stations, or the vast new *hypermarché*—even more enormous than a *supermarché*. We rushed past and out into the countryside, darting between fields of cherry trees and apple orchards and vineyards, onto the Route D2 and then, soon, onto the Nationale Cent—N100—the artery that connects us to the Vaucluse Valley, and home.

During the half-hour ride, I checked off landmarks:

• The gravel pit, just off to the left at the convergence of the D2 and the N100 near Cavaillon, a market town marked also as an exit off the Autoroute du Soleil superhighway running north-south past us to the Mediterranean

• Coustellet, a four-way stop and provisions mecca where we buy our daily croissants and baguette

• The caravan-park where rows of chubby recreation vehicles flaunt lace curtains in their rear windows

• Michael's favorite vegetable stand

And then the sign for Gordes, the nearest hill-village, which also comprises part of our summer address, and one hundred yards beyond, our turnoff—and the house.

I am home. I feel it. Even though this house does not belong to me, for one month it allows itself to be mine. I know its immediate bounds by heart, not just by rote.

Entering our village—a hamlet, really, of just a dozen dwellings—and the courtyard that separates us from the little graveled *place,* or village square, I could see that the house looks pristine. Moth said it had received a thorough rubdown by Philippe, Michael's new groundskeeper, and I could see this is so. Philippe, a potteryworker, scrubs the stone floors of the house, and waters the *pelouse*—our little swatch of lawn—and monitors the chemicals and filter for Michael's new *piscine*—a nine-stroke sliver of a swimming pool, in exchange for a tower room over Michael's own apartment overlooking our courtyard. Moth laughed in relief, since in other years, arriving in the wake of Michael's annual welcome-to-summer houseparty—one of the three visits he makes during the high season—she'd wallow in caches of abandoned bedclothes, congealed jams, and odd novels languishing, spine-up in mid-denouement, near the downstairs loo. This year, blissfully, she was able to dispose her photos and kitchen gadgets into perfectly ordered and clean rooms.

Like a trio of benevolent old lapdogs, we circled through the house to define our individual and private domains. Moth and Dad have ensconced themselves by habit, and because there are two of them and one of me, in the *toile de Jouy* double bedroom, with Moth's pink terry-cloth *pantoufle* flip-flop slippers and Dad's squashed-at-the-heel navy espadrilles parked side by side under a blanket rack.

I am across the landing in Michael's twin guest room, and Dad's closet-sized studio is between us. Through the doorway, spying his pencils tidily ground to perfect points next to his battery-operated sharpener and Casio keyboard, I could see that his sheaf of staff-lined sheet music already bore a scattered sprinkle of notes, a good heady rush into the Song Cycle he must complete over the next few weeks. Each summer his commission, large or small, dictates his routine—and accessibility. Sometimes he pursues the first melody line back home, but he's lucky this summer. The Song Cycle is short—and seems to have begun auspiciously, without his standard launching-into-work migraine.

In the interval since my last visit, Michael inherited what Moth calls "Mummy's *meubles*"—his mother's bedroom suite—which he entrusted to my room and care. Hearkening to a Louis XVI-esque ancestry, the skyblue-and-gilt ensemble overwhelms the small room in its variety and number: a pair of rocky cane-backed beds on wheels braked by a shallow jelly dish under each wheel; a narrow cheval mirror tilted so that it reflects, across the beds, an immense mirrored armoire insinuated into an alcove with less than an inch to spare; a tall skinny seven-drawer *semainier,* or lingerie chest; a dressing table, again mirrored but triptych-style; a pair of leggy bedtables; a luggage rack; assorted chairs. Extra pieces in the multifarious suite, including a huge dresser, overflow onto the landing. My first task, inevitably, would be to arrange this room so that I could install a work surface of sorts for a project I have been saving just for this sabbatical—

collages. And where would I jostle and jog through a daily Jane Fonda exercise tape?

After depositing my small hoard of clothing in the intimidating armoire—jumpers in a docile row on the pole, espadrilles and ballet shoes underneath—I reverted to ritual.

I needed, once again, to be blessed by this house. To feel at one with it, the first thing I do—always—is reacquaint my prim city-soft feet with its textures, testing touch, the most restrained of my five blunted senses. And so I removed my shoes and padded through the house, room by room and on outdoors.

My room—and all of upstairs—is paved in pale, blush-mottled clay tiles set within a gritty grid of concrete, and distressed here and there with branny frictions where the glaze didn't quite take. My soles, still tender from the train, flinched at the unaccustomed grain. Relax, I reminded myself; keep walking, or tiptoe if you must.

Then, from the upstairs hallway drops a grand stone stair which links the two stories of this house. The stair descends regally to an intermediary landing and then makes a left-hand turn down to the dim T of an entrance hall. Each pocked soapstone tread, coarsely scratched as if a rain had pummeled craters into its receptive skin, felt like emery board and scoured my feet. Each tread is so broad, too, that I must mince—always—in two sissy steps or risk one leap for each. The floor of the entrance hall, like that of the *salon*—the combination living/dining room it leads to down three more wide stairs—is blanketed in a fine, smooth palomino-hued local stone, like marble, and, like marble, it volunteers a perpetual and delicious cool underfoot. Cut in thick slices from a quarry we can see across the valley, the stones lock together in one seemingly seamless sweep. But when the stone extends out of the *salon,* through two sets of French doors, to the terrace, it submits to the corrosive kiss of wind and rain, and so is etched with lichen-like crust. Finally, returning through the hall to the kitchen, the floor changes yet again, to its most strictly utilitarian guise, a plebian red clay tile which feels in turn greasy or granular depending upon culinary accident.

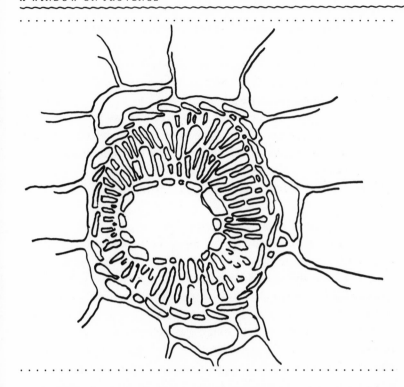

Out in the courtyard in front of the house, the gravel is interlarded with bands of smooth pebbles laid in orderly rows which demarcate our parking zone for the Souris. Bits of gravel clung to my too-soft toes and scattered across our welcome mat, itself composed of stones set into cement in a doughnut ring in front of the entranceway. In a month I can build sole pads of callus—then I'll barely feel the prick of gravel at all, and I will glide as easily over rock as over marble or tile.

The air chilled this evening so I drew a deep bath for warmth, added a drop of lavender oil from the essence distilled from our hamlet's annual harvest, and soaked, surrendering both to fragrance and to sound, as my feet had this afternoon to touch.

This bathroom amuses me. It opens, through an overscaled set of

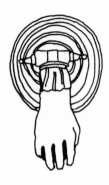

French doors, onto a tiny half-moon balcony encircled by a dainty wrought-iron railing. From the courtyard which it overlooks, the balcony gives an impression of grandeur, as if it cantilevered from a chamber worthy of Juliet rather than from a small, rather plain cubicle containing a precariously perched and quite plebeian clawfoot cast-iron tub. This architectural fillip overshadows the front door and is buttressed from below by a stone dolphin which rises in a high arc as if over a wave. We were told that the dolphin, mammal/ fish, symbolizes Christ and—along with a good-luck fisted knocker—blesses our house, granting happy fortune to all who enter here.

As I steeped in my bath, I felt indeed fortunate. Suddenly I recalled the dearest wish of a friend back in New York: Joan wants to swim with dolphins; she wants to feel her heartbeat pulse to dolphin song. I felt Joan's wish backstroke into my own as I rested. I felt my heartbeat pulse, and I felt myself sink into the sounds around this house.

Hearing touch and feeling sounds, as dolphins do: Joan's wish is mine—to be close to the place that resonates most truly to our senses. Here, I want to taste the air as much as food, to listen to my pencil as much as voice, to touch this place with the inside of my skin. I want my feet to speak words. I want to swim within this summer and hum the poetry of this house, without gasping for breath.

And just now, I wanted only to listen. Are the sounds I remember the same as before?

Outside, under the corduroy ridges of the rooftops, wasps and bees traded laconic drones back and forth to each other between fusillades into the lavender. Cicadas echoed their buzz, their violin-bow legs causing frissons of hum which will swell with increasing urgency as summer's heat intensifies. Tractors, parading the field-furrows in the distant downvalley past the lavender fields at the base of our hill ridge, purred as they aerated the twilit soil for irrigation and fertilizer; the farmers always ride out this task after the day's heat has dissipated. A mile or so distant, over on the N100, *camions* and cars whizzed by, accelerating fast into the straightaway that runs

from Coustellet to the vegetable stand, and then downshifting as they eased past the gas station in Les Beaumettes. And downstairs the fridge and the generator kept humming company like a pair of well-fed cats.

At this hour, too, the bi-plane man thrums in circles over the valley, up to Apt and across to the stone quarry and back towards Cavaillon. From my tub, I could see his little confection of a plane, an aerial red-and-blue go-cart strapped to gossamer wings, lights twinkling on the tail. He hangs, it seems, in a sort of sling beneath.

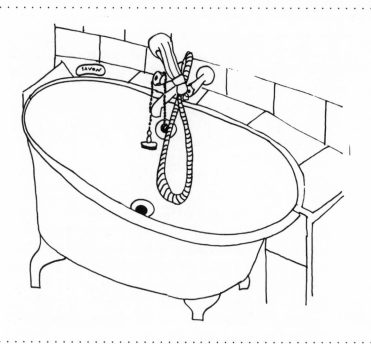

Tonight he kept up his buzzing until darkness forced him back to his hangar behind the caravan-park.

I hang too—somewhere between my American self and another, fantasy self. Released by sabbatical, released by permission into an extension of vacation as a gift of time from my boss, and a gift of distance—away from an office telephone or television or typewriter or copy machine—I feel emancipated from work, chameleon-like, reentering a self I once knew as a teenager when Europe first became part of me, when my parents themselves made a sabbatical, to Italy, to Florence, and into some new and foreign part of themselves.

Ostensibly we made that pilgrimage then to that particular place so that Dad, having played jazz piano in nightclubs in New York, could try his hand at classical piano and composing. A teacher of orchestration was recommended to him, and my mother, intuiting the frustrations of the nightclub scene, had a dream: of Florence, and of testing themselves within the context of another place, where they had only one friend and no language at all.

It seemed incredible perhaps to move back then, in the late 1950s, away from the safety net of two conservative families and our school. But devoting our lives to Dad's music seemed an amiable adventure just then, when my parents approached mid-life, and it would be an affordable adventure too because Dad came into a liberating though not lavish inheritance, a trust fund that might allow him a year or two to explore his future.

So we went.

Why we were there evolved into an unnecessary question before the sabbatical year expired. Florence was by luck gloriously affordable. So we moved from one low-cost rental into another and yet another; my parents adroitly prolonged their stay to a dozen years.

After attending the American one-room school—run by an antiquated Bostonian spinster émigrée who had sat out World War II with her fencing lance upon her knee—for a couple of grades, we children were flown back to complete our education in America. But we spent summers in Florence, and the question for us of why we returned resolved itself with each visit: We are here and we remain here because we are happy. My father began to write his music and my mother to paint and to photograph, and we three sisters began, quite simply, to grow up.

In Florence, we grew out of the confines of parental rule and into our own lives. We began to learn something of another place and other people. We fell in love with art and with music. We attended opera night after summer night for 600 lira (80 cents then) a ticket, standing room, and devoured pizzas and *gelati* and danced under umbrella pines at a club beyond the city walls. We sang. We lay, side by side, with gangs of passing-through-town friends on our tiled roof and told stories. We teetered on two languages and slid back and forth within our chameleon identities, as Americans in Florence and as *stranieri*—foreigners, and sometimes strangers, too—in America.

Finally we all—first us sisters, one by one, and then my parents—

returned to America to live. But we continue to feel the tug of our European ties. Moth and Dad annually budget a summer sojourn, a reprieve from homebound obligations, into their year.

This summer, too, I have released myself from home, taken my own reprieve. This is a sabbatical from work, but a sabbatical from home too, from the responsibilities of being a wife and a mother, time just for me, to look and listen, to read and do collages and to write, and to simply stop the continuum for a few weeks. It is a time to reconnect with my childhood in the company of my parents, and a time to reconnect with my childhood in an environment I have missed.

It is difficult, I can tell, for Bill and David and Peter to understand my urgency to spend this time abroad and away, even though they are occupied, and even after their two visits here with me, but they supported my desire: Go.

9 *July*

Five-thirty A.M.: At this shadowy juncture between dawn and day, a shuddering, penetrating chill mantles our house. Like the Arizona desert, the Vaucluse Valley awakens and slumbers to sweatshirt cool, only simmering to pulsating heat by early afternoon. Even the cock sleeps in, tucking feathers tight. Day unfolds in slow motion.

Out my window, dim, as yet indeterminate, shapes begin to transform into the view I've come to love so well. I feel as if I were back in the darkroom I haunted after college, encouraging a hazy image forth from negative film to positive photo, from bleeding blur into focused scene.

The Vaucluse—the Romans named this place the *vallis clausa,* or closed valley—interpenetrates two mountain ranges. Behind us and out of sight of our village towers the emphatic, implacable, sinister bald-pated grayish hulk of Mont Ventoux and pine-dappled ancillary ridges which ripple east and north towards the Drôme. South, across the valley and on the other side of the N100, stretches the gentler recumbent but bony hogback of the forested Petit Lubéron and, upvalley, the Grand. Off to the west, beyond the Autoroute du Soleil, I can just make out the outline of the Alpilles; the spiky spine of their stegosaurus silhouette today shimmers in mist, signaling heat to come.

As the sun commences its stately ascent into day, its rays glide like tawny drizzles of syrup down the furrowed flank of the Lubéron to spill into the gaping, wan, and now-extinct quarry, exposed like jawbone, where the pale stones for our hall and *salon* were gathered.

Eye level with our house, against the Lubéron's protective haunch, erupt a pair of truncated ridges, small buttes really, upon which rest two of our favorite *villages perchés,* or hill-villages, Ménerbes and Oppède-le-Vieux. Every morning the sun first grazes the rooftops of Ménerbes and then, moments later, fingers the more modestly scaled dwellings of Oppède. Once both villages are bathed in light, the sun begins its leisurely stroll towards our house, high-stepping over the vine-streaked valley floor, then, row by row, across the banks of luxuriant lavender which, like puffy chenille fringes, border our village. The lavender, suffused with new light, awakens to a deep intense violet, almost blue, that rivals the sky.

The sun finally nuzzles our little oasis of a garden. Because of a long wet spring, the garden has blossomed into explosive billows of leaf and bloom. Normally by July our postage-stamp lawn withers to a crewcut of prickly crabgrass, exposing freckles of parched earth to the searing sun. This year the lawn, a plush carpet, must—at least so far—be mowed twice weekly. Even the magnolia tree at the corner of the terrace and the roses climbing the stone walls enclosing the garden are still profusely petaled.

Unfortunately one discordant note mars this symphony of verdant abundance. Moth wrote last year that one of the three elegant cypresses which anchor the far end of the garden seemed tainted with disease, and this year a stubborn blotch of decay indeed defiles the center tree; its entire left side looks as if torched by fire. We've heard from friends that a virulent scourge, like Dutch elm disease, is decimating the cypresses throughout Italy; I can't bear to think that these will succumb as well. Without the cypresses our view of the Lubéron would be sadly diminished.

Our house, before it ever was a house, had been a shed, part of a farm complex which—like countless others in this region—supplied thread to a once-flourishing silk industry north of us in Lyons. When Michael bought the shed twenty-five years ago at the suggestion of a friend who is also a neighbor, it had been long abandoned. A faded, crumpled snapshot in his visitors book reveals a nondescript three-walled structure, its sloping tiled roof supported by a thick round column. Today, two clues allude to the history of this shed: A giant mulberry shades our courtyard, reminding us of the diet of the voracious silkworms; and inside the house, large holes punctuate the side walls of our bedrooms, indicating where long poles used for hanging silken thread once straddled the rooms.

When Michael launched his overhaul of the shed, he sliced into its steeply sloping earthen floor to create the ground-floor rooms and to connect the courtyard to the garden. At the top of the slope, which was level with the courtyard, he placed the entrance to the house and a deep front hall, and, off the hall, the kitchen, a diminutive rarely used formal dining room, and a bath. Three wide stone steps drop into the *salon,* which itself lies on two levels. The upper, furnished with a long oak refectory table flanked by two benches, and a buffet, can accommodate up to a dozen diners comfortably. Michael reserved the lower level for his "conversation pit," near a wine cellar he hid behind armoire doors built right into the wall.

Here an enormous provençal fireplace and chimneypiece of pitted sandstone decorated with a carved thistle warms the room during Michael's winter visits, but during our summers, when the fireplace stands idle, its thick wrought-iron andirons prop a thick sheaf of aromatic lavender stalks in lieu of logs. Two chubby roll-arm *canapés,* or sofas, and a pair of matching easy chairs surround the hearth. Until this year they used to be draped in slouchy covers of nubbly blue cotton which, bearing the strain of years of lounging house-guests, had collapsed at their seams. Each summer, in exasperation, Dad basted fat stitches across the most furious rips and shreds—but this year Michael must have demurred to comradely pressure, because the covers have vanished and instead we can recline against taut-welted upholstery in a sporty yellow-and-green provençal print. We feel quite decorated.

Before my arrival Moth positioned her writing table between the pairs of French doors leading to the terrace and marched her row of summer reading books behind her blotter. Her plan this summer is to read all of Trollope, but in undertaking this project, she has abandoned her paints and I shall miss her watercolors. One of the projects of past family visits was to entrap insects for her still lifes. An incentive of a franc per bug galvanized the village children, who joined David and Peter on a quest for the most vicious-looking rhinoceros beetles they could find. These two-inch-long blue-black critters with crooked horns joined her exotic menagerie—dung-hued scorpions flailing menacing poison-tipped deviltails, hairy-legged spiders, and translucent butterflies—under hatpins pushed into Styrofoam sorbet containers.

One of Moth's insect studies folds out of the visitors book, a gift and souvenir of our earliest stay of four summers ago. The *salon,* in fact, is a gallery of souvenirs, renditions of house and village in all media, courtesy of houseguests-turned-artists. Against the backdrop of troweled stucco walls we count a half-dozen framed artworks: the village square in oil and in pastel; the courtyard in watercolor and again in ink; the chimneypiece in gouache; and even an oil portrait of Michael himself, ruddy and cheerful, ever the charming host.

As far as villages or hamlets go, ours is tiny, indeed so small we have no church and no market square, no bar or café, no post office and no *boulangerie,* or bakery, none of the amenities which characterize a classic French village. Most of the dwellings which compose our *hameau* cluster around the *place,* a graveled oblong just broad enough to embrace a handful of cars, an ancient well, a stone bench, and, in years past, a Sunday afternoon round of *petanque* or *boules—* the provençal version of bowling, where contestants hurl heavy metal balls at a nut.

Our hamlet undoubtedly expanded upon an extended farmstead, for some of the other houses besides ours had also once bustled with silkworms. We boast our own "château," a stern, stucco-veneered manor of refined silhouette and regal bearing whose unadorned pediment can be seen from some distance down the road. Once there was a bakery too: a beehive oven dominates the living room in the house of our American neighbor, Peggy, who summers on the far side of the château.

From the square, our hamlet appears no different on the surface from others of its size or type which dot the valley. Its houses present reserved shuttered façades—or façades with no windows at all—to the square; any gardens or terraces or balconies, where families congregate, radiate to the rear and elude public scrutiny. One can live here, and many do, in absolute isolation. Those of us who know each other, and are acquaintances or friends as well as neighbors, visit—but only after a *coup de téléphone*—for we all seek calm and privacy.

The composition of our hamlet is deceptive in its simplicity. Many of the buildings share walls or rooftops which overlap or interlock, stone to stone and tile to tile, in quirky montage. Michael's studio hovers over a storage shed, and interfaces with Philippe's tower, which in turn slides atop the bedroom of a landscape gardener, Jacques, whose daughter Agnès's bedroom links with an arch that connects to the room David and Peter occupied. We never know quite where one house begins or ends.

The three dwellings standing together along the north side of the *place* appear to be separated one from the other, but we don't know for certain if that is true. At the center hunches a mysterious and brooding house that suggests human habitation only by the occasional dogbark from behind its enormous, solemn, and tight-lipped doorway constructed of mismatched weathered planks studded with nails. To its left and linked, like a parenthesis, by a splinter of a court—dressed, under a canopy of bamboo shoots and vine, with a red-and-white checkered cloth-draped table and four rush-seated side chairs—rises a narrow three-story tower punctuated by three windows, one stacked atop the other, but none aligned. The top window, sheltered by a diminutive tiled overhang, staggers a bit to the left, and a pillow perpetually droops over its sill. A small shed protrudes from the hip of the tower into a graveled path, barely wide enough for a car to pass through, which leads up out of the hamlet past two goose pens, a cement-sided duck pond, and the local *chambre d'hôte,* or B-&-B. To the right of the brooding house, and set back deferentially behind a low row of stones and paved laundry yard where baby buntings and diapers flap on the line, a smaller house squats behind half-closed shutters. This house also faces the second village egress, which passes alongside the local honeyman's compound and shop.

The honeyman raises bees nearby and manufactures several varieties of honey which he sells here, but also from a large, quite touristy shop up in Gordes. In the village his ancillary boutique, flagged with a SONNEZ ICI/RING HERE shutter, catches the eye of the occasional automobile passing along the country road above our village. We buy our own honey here rather than in Gordes; Moth favors the Milles-Fleurs sweet granular spread while I prefer the more pungent tang of thick creamy-toned Lavender. After sampling earthy Rosemary and woodsy Oak, we concur these are too robust for our palates.

The amalgam of dwellings along the south side of the *place*—our complex, the château, which belongs to a Belgian family, Peggy's bakery and her daughter Sarah's mule shed and another low-lying silkworm factory—joins friends with a commitment in common. All

foreigners, but none from the same country, the friends had met abroad during a coinciding tenure in international business and diplomacy and agreed to purchase, as a consortium, the swath of lavender we see from our windows. They thus protect the land and mutual view from development.

The automobiles in our hamlet have established unmarked priority parking zones according to need. The casual observer would deem the arrangement haphazard, as the cars seem to position themselves at random; but each, in fact, slips precisely into a preordained spot: Jacques's landscaping truck resides in the shade of a large tree near the well; Peggy's white Citroën parallels Sarah's shed; Philippe's battered Renault nudges his tower stair; our Souris rests alongside the mulberry tree in our courtyard, but out of range of its moist and sticky fruit-droppings; and Michael's British Mini berths under an arch.

Dogs, too, demarcate their territory. The village mayor and his wife bundle a trio of feisty curs of indeterminate origin in their farmstead down at the other end of the village past the house that harbors a *chien méchant,* a ferocious Doberman-like barking menace that must be tethered at all times. The Belgians' Miró, an immense

fuzzy black dog whom we favored, sadly died of old age over the winter and his pride of place has been assumed by Apollon, a lanky hunting breed resembling a cross between a terrier and a dachshund that bespeaks impeccable credentials hearkening back, Michael tells us, four centuries. Apollon actually resides in a house across the single-lane county road which separates our hamlet from another up the hill, but he dignifies this village with his regal presence as if it were his own. We presume that his benediction results from his love affair with Michael, who cajoles him into our house with nibbles and a water bowl always filled for his refreshment. Michael, indeed, admonishes us to change the water daily, and so we do, and we are rewarded with the tick-tick of Apollon's toenails at least twice daily, and a contented slurp.

Thus, we co-exist. Although we heard of a rift between two neighbors over a supposedly rancid bottle of olive oil and although we obviously avoid the *chien méchant,* we discern little this summer to upset the amicable calm. There is an illness in the village this summer, though, too, which mutes both voices and activities. The village mayor is dying; we respect the silence.

Still, I cannot help but remember the sounds from the square. Our first summer here, Peter had become a sort of village mascot to the mayor, Papa Roger, and his wife, Mme. V., and to Jacques and his family; and he would disappear every evening into one house or the other to watch game shows on television or accompany Mme. V. when she fed Papa Roger's nanny goat. Peter was the youngest child in the village that summer, and the family gathered him in as if he were one of their own.

Then, too, our Belgian neighbors had their grandsons in residence, and David and Peter would slip over our mutual wall to swim in their pool or set up an independent game of *boules* in their driveway just beyond the archway that separates our courtyard from their gate or, at dusk, play endless rounds of *touche-touche* tag around the sleeping cars in the square.

Agnes shared her Smurfs—or "Schtroumpfs"—with the boys, and they all chattered and rattled about in the boys' own secret apartment,

which Peggy called the *oubliette,* "forgotten" under the arch. They
felt so grown up with their own house away from ours. One room
up and one down, it tucked into a niche carved into one corner of
the Belgian château—we could see their kitchen window overhead—
and it abutted a storage alcove where Jacques deposited Mimi, the
cat, when the family went off for a Sunday drive.

STORIES OF OUR VILLAGE

Courtship

Monsieur V.—Papa Roger—went away from this valley to complete his military service in the mountains, and while there met a soldier of his own age who carried a photograph of his sister in his breastpocket. Curious, Papa Roger inquired: 'Who is she? And then—perhaps exchanged a letter or two?—but finally made a visit to her village and observed her as she served customers in the local café. Immediately he asked: Would she marry him? And she accepted—on the condition that he, an atheist, convert to Catholicism. Which he duly did—but only through the wedding, whereupon he reverted to his own opinions, and he held to them, surely and steadfastly, ever after.

The Christmas Goat

One Christmas, Papa Roger arranged for a young billy goat to come to the village to make a union with his own little nanny. On the very morning of the holiday, as the turkey was revolving gently upon the spit, he drove away to fetch the billy and soon returned with it sitting in the back seat of his automobile. The billy, sadly, took no notice of the nanny, and turned aside to seek a thistle. Papa Roger, outraged, pushed at the billy and prodded him, and pushed him again to consummate the union. The turkey, continuing to turn as the assembled guests looked on, began to lose its luster. And the guests began to feel rumblings of hunger. But still Papa Roger persisted. At long last, *victoire!* But then the billy refused to leave the nanny alone and he refused to get back into the automobile. Pushing and prodding recommenced, and darkness fell upon the festivities—and upon a dry turkey too.

10 July, Sunday

Our kitchen, a dark oblong room with two small windows, one facing the courtyard and a blooming bougainvillaea and the other the laundry line and a massive pine, comes fully equipped, but with an eccentric conglomeration of appliances which appear to have been flung into centrifugal spin to plug in, at random, wherever they came into contact with a wall. Michael's friends who attend his regular houseparties throughout the year concur that his kitchen tests their loyalty, especially an encounter with the Old Dowager, an aging and diabolical gas stove with a reputation for singeing eyebrows. The Dowager was known to bow to none but Michael; when his friends happen to encounter each other they do not exchange greetings but rather compare eyebrow scars.

We'd heard rumors that the Dowager had been retired at long last, and it has turned out to be true. Docile and obedient, a petite new range winks benignly into flame.

The fridge this year is also new, a surprise for us, and thus relieves Dad of his twice-weekly defrostings. This sedate new model respectfully coddles our myriad cheeses, sorbets, yoghurts, and juices, with nary a hint of frost. The old fridge, unplugged and banished to the laundry shed, stares balefully at us as we pass by on our way out to the vegetable garden; she hoards vintage wines in her dark maw.

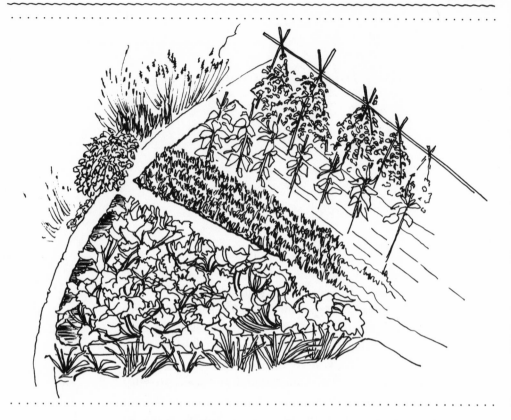

Our garden spreads into a graceful fan shape a few steps down from the kitchen and laundry line. A bit of boxwood secures the base of the fan, while a leafy stand of bamboo protects the northwest border from grunting mistral winds which hurtle into our valley from the mountains. The tallest plants cluster near the bamboo and then telescope down in size and volume to the most delicately petaled lettuces bordering the path leading down past the garden to the pool. Slender poles of dried bamboo, crossed like swords and tied with twine, support this summer's crop of tomatoes. Philippe attends to all the makings of a ratatouille in our garden: the tomatoes, onions, zucchini or *courgettes,* peppers, eggplant. We also have sorrel, a favorite leaf of Michael's, his requisite green beans, and a variety of herbs—basil, rosemary, thyme, chives. Under the laundry line, a thick clump of mint flourishes.

Because all the plantings in our garden are still immature, we decided to forage for luncheon at the weekly farmers' market which is held every Sunday down in Coustellet. Although many villages host a weekly market, rotating day to day throughout the valley and beyond, and although the atmosphere of each is defined by the character of its particular locale, the merchandise rarely varies: foods, clothing both antique and colorfully bizarre, funky jewelry, pottery, baskets, books, kitchen gadgets. Only Coustellet holds a pure farmers' market, exhibiting fruits and vegetables, herbs and flowers, plus compatible *saucissons* and cheeses and, of course, honey. Sunday dinner evolves from market produce, delicious and perfectly fresh.

Moth insinuated the Souris into a barely perceptible parking spot alongside the fringe of the *brocantes,* or flea market, spread out behind the *"pressing"* dry cleaners and across from the newly expanded deli. I've always considered Moth curiously blessed by some magic Parking Angel, as everywhere she goes a place miraculously vacates as she creeps by. But perhaps she has simply learned from the habit of the French, who create *"parkings"* wherever convenient—driving up onto sidewalks, stalling in the middle of the street, or just shutting off the ignition wherever they happen to be.

As the new fridge requires a butter dish, we made a preliminary prowl of the *brocantes* before crossing over to the market. A collision of objects spilling over a table and onto the ground in casual disarray attracted us to one dealer, who squinted at us from his deck chair in the shade of a bamboo hedge. Surrounding him in bizarre counterpoint lurked a stuffed badger baring its fangs, a pair of luridly embossed ceramic wishing wells, a thickly encrusted and garishly hued "artistic" oil rendition of a fishing village *à la* van Gogh or perhaps Monet, and a miscellany of kitchenwares tumbled over a threadbare rug. From the heap we upended a chunky glass butter dish, perfect for the fridge, and after a brief haggle it was ours for 10 francs, or about $1.75.

Crossing the main street which is also the N100, we headed into the usually empty lot behind the Banque Agricole and the deli. The lot was now crowded to capacity with *camions* drawn up into a ring, like stagecoaches, opening aft to umbrella-shaded displays set out in crates and boxes on folding tables. It is easy to understand why Provence is renowned as the garden of France, as all summer long these markets spill over with a profusion of seemingly endless harvest. We find the colors and textures and fragrance almost overwhelming, but the bounty is harnessed by an innate sensibility to design. Each fruit, each vegetable, each potted herb, each bunch of flowers, prettily disposed in its fabric- or plastic-lined basket or crate or bin seems ennobled, dignified, honored for its precious individuality.

We inquired after peaches *biens mûrs,* or ripe for today, and a selection was made for us, each peach presented for our inspection like a gift to be remarked upon and admired. Reacting with some inbred New York paranoia or perhaps just a simple distrust of a sales pitch, we caught ourselves having to rein in our impulse to contradict our vendor, to touch and test the peaches for ourselves. Stop and smile—wait, she said, until you prepare them for the repast, don't touch them now.

Peaches bobbing in our *filet,* or string bag, a requisite for shopping without grocery carts, we pushed on into the throngs. It appears we are the only foreigners here today; others undoubtedly will attend these markets as summer progresses and holiday houses fill for vacation.

We bypassed the sausages, selecting instead a thick slab of ham to share and then made our way to the cheese cart to choose a goat cheese, or chèvre, a specialty of the mountains east of Apt. And what chèvres! Chèvres wrapped in leaves. Chèvres flagged with round target labels. Chèvres dusted with pepper, fine or coarse. Chèvres molded into tiny patties, spooned into thimble domes, paddled into pyramids. Chèvres both dry and flaky or sticky-moist. Moth zeroed in on a Banon, from the town of the same name.

Returning home, we assembled our lunch like a collage: salad,

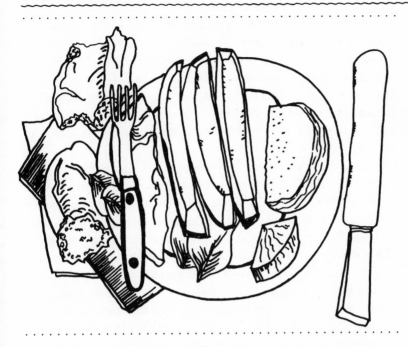

crusty bread or crackers with the Banon, fruit—today, of course, the peaches—and, for a sweet, Délices Chocs, biscuits coated with rich bittersweet chocolate. Eating simply of seasonal produce, just what happens to be up in the garden or in the market or offered to us by friends, satisfies us. While here we do not long for innovation, for variety, for complexity, for sauces or fancy accompaniments. We do not long for restaurants, really, although we always plan a couple of outings to taste the local cuisine and to enjoy the beautiful settings in this region. Preparing these simple lunches every day soothes us and turns us into addicts for plain fare. I can never satiate my taste for a garden-ripened tomato.

To fill out our household necessities, we headed over in the late afternoon to L'Isle-sur-la-Sorgue a few miles down the N100, and to its supermarket. The *supermarché* has assumed a new identity since I was here last; it is no longer known as the Lion Codec, but rather the Système U, with ironic, pseudopolitical banners, actually marketing ploys, extolling Solidarity and Unity. Despite this sweeping declaration, the *super* seems much the same. Only the Système for shopping carts reveals a new managerial dictate. The carts, locked together in ranks around the parking lot, cannot be removed without introducing a ten-franc coin into a special slot, thus releasing the cart—as in airports—and when the cart is returned, the coin pops back out.

As always, I was drawn into the *super* like an iron shaving to a magnet because I love to review the energetic graphics, the animated packaging designs, and the tactics of display. But Moth wheeled our cart first to a stash of outdoor furniture next to the sliding glass entrance. Each year Moth and Dad make a project of purchasing two chairs for the terrace or pool, and the assemblage at the house is, after six years, most interesting. Two gridded mesh stacking chairs led the pack joined, on subsequent vacations, by twin iron bentwoods, two slatted plastic folding chairs, and two carry-around canvas beach chairs among others. Today Moth opted for two new wooden slatted chairs to pull around the outdoor dining table.

Like a trained patrol, we work the market. Anticipating a houseparty Michael has corralled for Bastille Day just four days hence, Dad investigated the beverage bins for wines and mineral waters while Moth swept through the aisles of breakfast jams and conserves and biscuits. I rounded up the necessary bath soaps, tissues, paper towels, and sundries, and then, freed of obligation, scouted small gifts to take home to Bill and the boys and my in-laws. Small commonplace objects that differ from their counterparts at home please me the most as gifts, but what to choose? Beachballs tossed into an enormous plastic pail are altogether too large to carry home; the T-shirts altogether too lurid. Next to the *poubelles,* or garbage cans, polka-dotted bikini panties, for women and for men, were tugged on over anatomically correct cardboard buttocks, while multistriped socks kicked up alongside in Rockette rank. Espadrilles made in Taiwan cost half of those made locally.

Cruising the aisles, my eye was caught by labels:

> PHÉNIX is a lemonade
> POUPIE is a grape juice
> REALDRINK is a beverage containing exotic fruits
> SCHWEPPES is also called DRY EXOTIC
> PIROUETTE is a crême fraîche
> GLORIA is an evaporated milk
> YOP and YOCO are yoghurts
> PEAUDOUCE and LOTUS are tissues

By the time we reconvened at the check-out, I had gathered an armful of family gifts: insecticide-impregnated cardboard sticks to bury in flowerpots for my mother-in-law's sunroom; tablecloth clips for my father-in-law's picnic table; palm-tree-patterned briefs for Bill to jog in if he dares; a paddle-and-spongeball set for David, and a miniature Peugeot 405 for Peter to add to his collection of French cars.

This year shrinkwrapping seems to have overtaken the *super* and so even as I inwardly criticize the American penchant for encasing everything in plastic, I am perturbed to think the French will capitulate to the same urge. An elderly man precedes us through the check-out bearing two baguettes shining in plastic wrap—I never thought the fresh-today baguette could be desanctified—and Dad pushes through his own shrinkwrapped *occasion,* or sale item, a four-pack of local rosé at 20 francs.

11 July

Dichotomies: The land of Provence changes so abruptly from one mile to the next—from deep and twisted gorges contorted with jagged stone and stunted pine, to placid vine-braceleted hillsides; from crunchy moonscape *garrigues,* or heaths, strewn with scabby boulders to sea-splotched salt marsh; from tree-mantled mountain ridges to patchwork plains—it is as if God merely squeezed this small parcel of Earth and patted it into place, just in passing, on His way to grander or broader horizons.

James Pope-Hennessy, British biographer and travel writer, wrote in his 1952 portrait *Aspects of Provence,* in words both atmospheric and acerbic, that this region is "drenched in human living," and so it seems to be. Provence, on the way to so many places—Italy, Spain, Switzerland, North Africa—has endured conquest, invasion, and infiltration, and its history is rife with attack, with persecution, with raids and rapes, with torture and torment—as well as bold construction and architectural and cultural achievement.

Colonists from Greek Asia Minor were the first *étrangers,* or foreigners, to settle in Provence, and many writers still rhapsodize about the classic Greek profile of many a woman of Arles. I am untutored in resemblances, so I simply take this information on faith. The Romans, extending their influence throughout Europe, established themselves here, of course, in this land-next-door, employing Greek workmen to build for them. The Roman ruins scattered throughout "Provincia"—Latin for province and now Provence—attest to their fine workmanship, and are the biggest tourist draw these days, after the beaches of the Riviera, because the Provençaux simply absorbed the constructions and let them be. Closest to our house stands the tiny single-arched Pont Julien, a slip of a bridge arching over a fetid creek; the more famous Pont du Gard straddles a small river over on the far side of the Autoroute du Soleil, and north of Avignon. Amphitheaters in Arles and in Nîmes and a magnificent theater in Orange and the ruins of an entire town in Vaison-la-Romaine all bear witness to Roman rule.

Hannibal made a rest stop here, feeding and watering his elephants before his assault on the Alps. And who else? Visigoths, absorbing the best of what was Roman, and then, turning north, taking on the Franks. The Visigoths educated themselves to Roman law and learned the new Christian religion too, but they preferred the warlike demeanor of the Frankish perception of Christ to a dovish spiritual version. The Frankish "code of chivalry," marked by selfishness and superstition, allowed for sacking, raping, and looting.

In the ninth century, Charlemagne placed lieutenants in charge of his outlying provinces and thus established the feudal system, with lords owning land and passing it on to the eldest son, and peasants and serfs supported the system.

The twelfth century interposed an era of calm into the generally violent sequence of invasions. This was a period of *gentille courtoisie,* as well as a time of commerce, of so-called courtly love and refinement. There was bounty and food for everyone, games and dances, poetry, and good manners and kindness. This was the era of the troubadour, or wandering balladeer, who entertained the feudal court with long song-poems, a time when local lords rode forth into the forest while their gentlewomen, left behind, worked at the needlecrafts or, as many *chansons,* or songs, declare, took lovers. Saints and heroes and even children possessing ususual reserves of strength populate the medievel tales—many of which are lovingly reenacted at local fêtes throughout the summer today.

THREE MEDIEVAL TALES

The Legend of La Tarasque

Tarascon, later the home of Provence's beloved Good King Réné, had been—long, long ago—under siege to a terrible dragon called by the townspeople La Tarasque. The saintly Martha—who had arrived, it is said, on the shore of Provence on a boat in the company of the sister of the Virgin Mary and Mary Magdalene, as well as their Egyptian slave girl, Sara—was living in Tarascon at the time. Martha took herself to the mouth of the cave wherein dwelt La Tarasque and, speaking softly to the great beast, admonished it to come out—in the Name of the Lord. The dragon, hearing her gentle voice, came to the doorway. Bending its neck in submission, it breathed its now-quiet breath upon her. Martha removed the sash girdling her waist and placed it around the neck of La Tarasque and, tugging at the sash like a leash, led the dragon into the city. Whereupon it was slain before the townspeople—and before God.

Aucassin and Nicolette

Aucassin, son of the count of Beaucaire—the city facing Tarascon across the Rhône—fell in love with a slave girl brought to his city by Saracen pirates. Aucassin's father, horrified, declared that his son would descend into Hell if he loved the slave girl outside the bond of marriage—but he would not condone a union. Aucassin entered into an argument with his father: Why should he aspire to Heaven if he could not have his beloved by his side? Everyone who ascends to Heaven, he continued, is either maimed or crippled or, worst of all, desiccated, like a monk. Everyone entering Hell, by contrast, is brave: knights and soldiers who lost their lives in battle and ladies who resigned themselves to loving others because their own lords neglected them. He, Aucassin, would rather be with those in Hell because they had spirit. Aucassin's father, angered to the core, placed his son and his true love in prison. They escaped and endured many tribulations. At the end of the long tale, Nicolette is discovered to be a princess and the couple—at last—marry happily.

How the Cliffs of Roussillon
Turned the Color of Blood

Once there lived a lord, the lord of Roussillon, who was called by name Raymond d'Avignon. So enamoured was he of the hunt that he spent all of his days—each day from dawn until dusk—roaming far and wide, across the *garrigues* far from his village, in pursuit of the wild beast. His wife, Sermonde, left alone, was consoled by a young troubadour, Guillaume, who lived at the château. Raymond learned of their affair and became irate. Concealing his rage from his wife, he invited Guillaume to join him one day at the hunt, and after riding some distance from the château, turned upon him and had him killed and torn into pieces. When Raymond returned that evening, he called for Sermonde and invited her to dine with him. Complimenting her upon her beauty, he served her the most succulent morsels from his own plate, and with his own hand. After she had finished, he told her that she had nibbled upon the very heart of her lover. Sermonde rose at once from her chair and declared to everyone gathered there that she had eaten well, and forever. As she spoke she sprang to the edge of the cliff outside the banquet hall and threw herself from it. Just at the spot where she landed, a spring gushed forth. All the countryfolk who lived nearby erected a well around the spring to protect Sermonde and her love from the rage of jealous men. And her blood tinged the cliffs all around, red-ocher, showing ever after that her love was strong and eternal.

Courtoisie did not last long, however, and Provence was stricken once again by struggle, and especially by religious conflict, which pitted Protestant against Catholic in a series of bloodbaths that scarred both land and soil more brutally and more deeply than any foreign war. Town battled town, guerrilla-like, and family fought family. Provence was ripped apart by persecution.

Invasion. Conquest. Persecution. We find it difficult to imagine such atrocities while we bask in our "simple life."

Frédéric Mistral, a provençal poet who attempted to revive this region's native tongue, reveled in the contradictions of his neighbor Provençaux. He spent twenty years compiling and writing a dictionary of the dialect, called the langue d'oc, and shared the Nobel Prize in 1904 for his literary efforts. In four long poems he embraced the dichotomies: the generous with the heedless, the tender with the crude, the impassioned with the sensible. He sang the songs of his beloved Provençaux in full voice, in expletives—and prayed with his knees firmly embedded in the soil.

This langue d'oc derived from a late and vulgarized Latin spoken here; a more mellifluous tongue, the langue d'oïl took root closer to Paris and, in 1539, was decreed by the government to be the official language of France.

Today the twang of dialect, though, still lives on in Provence, spicing the French. Burly and boisterous, earthy and juicy, Provençal, like the Provençaux, is indeed a gutsy, physical language.

Just the other day, we happened upon a scene that could have unfolded like a living tableau of dichotomies. Saturdays in July, we learned, are devoted to weddings which occur, one after the other, throughout the afternoon. Following the rhythmic peals of church bells echoing out of the cathedral in L'Isle-sur-la-Sorgue, we arrived in the main square just as a young bride and her groom emerged, laughing, onto the cathedral steps. Holding hands, they ran down the steps into the raucous, riotous embrace of their families and into a lipstick-red Peugeot all decked out in lace like a big bonbon. Each door handle, the antenna, the rearview mirror, and the license plates were all tied up in fat white-lace bows. Wide lace ribbon wrapped the car completely from hood to trunk, pulled up into a festive topknot grasping a nosegay of shiny plastic flowers. More plastic flowers filled the car.

As we approached, watching the bridal pair with much prodding and chatter enter their car, another wedding party entered the square. No one noticed their arrival until they were almost upon the car, for they marched in rank, two by two, in utter silence. At the head of the procession walked the bride, no more than sixteen, stiff in lace-encrusted tulle, eyes cast down. Clutching her arm, equally grave, strode who? her father—not her husband-to-be, surely—perhaps sixty, his hair, white and stiff and prickled, his face weathered and devoid of emotion, his suit, serviceable, gray, unadorned. Was she being led inexorably into a marriage against her will?

When we lived in Florence, arranged marriages were commonplace; I did not believe that in this place at this time history would be so ingrained as to still hold such rituals.

A British writer, Julian More, whose *View from a French Farmhouse* sits on our coffeetable, censures the foreign affectation of the Simple Life where summer visitors play at the "barefoot *paysan*" in requisite provençal-patterned skirts, lace-embellished camisoles, headscarves, farmers' smocks, espadrilles.

I frankly admit to bare feet. I joyfully don my summer costume of a loose-fitting jumper. I purchase my espadrilles and will wear them until they are ragged at their heel-flattened backs. I bring ballet shoes for dress-up so that I can feel the stones I walk on through their thin soles. Perhaps I'll find at the market some more Day-Glo throwaway faux-silk pumps like the ones I bought four years ago for five francs, and another straw hat.

We think, What of it? Living as a foreigner in a foreign place, as so many writers describe, is a confrontation, perhaps, between what is supposedly real about a vacation, and what is fantasy. We find it blissful to live another life here—it touches our senses so.

We recall our years in Florence and Tuscany. As artists abroad, my parents granted themselves an unspoken permission—to live as they wanted, without censure. To other foreigners there, we hovered somewhere between Ambassador and Bohemian. Our house, with its levels of terraces and rooftops and even a garret studio, became

42

an informal annex to our local consulate and a hub for any kids traveling through. We were *stranieri,* but the Florentines, through the introduction of a childhood friend of Dad's who married one, tolerated us, even liked us. Dad rowed a scull on the Arno River with policemen and shopkeepers. Moth gave "tossed salad" parties for whoever cared to come. We were curiosities, perhaps, but we always felt completely at home.

As we do here. We have some friends here, foreigners like ourselves, and a few French. The bare feet feel right and good. The sun is hot and the air is dry and the food is fresh and the wine, sharp and tangy and cheap. If these things conspire to make us happy with the Simple Life, we can't resist!

12 *July*

Today, following Dad's lead, I disciplined myself to a morning indoors to make a start at collages. Collages strike my fancy; I've long been attracted both to their sense of design and to their resilience to shades of humor as well as serious intent. I like the idea of mixing up media, mingling the painterly with the architectonic, pencil, say, with magazine scrap. On our last trip, David and Peter, both architecturally inclined too, joined me in making some collages because, like jigsaws or building blocks, collages encourage a pursuit that works both as project and as a game much like a scavenger hunt. Together we linked shards and snips, color forms and words, daubs of paint and odd little found objects into playful constructions.

Upon return home that year, I remembered our games and turned again to collages, but less to play with than as an exercise in design. This summer I wanted to look into them yet again, to delve deeper into them, to find the art, rather than just the craft, that might connect the bits, to see what might ultimately emerge if I allowed enough time.

I brought eight thick square cards the color and texture of oatmeal as backgrounds for a first series—patchworks of windowpane shards outlined with penciled stitches—which I will call Window Quilts. It's best, I believe, to go at them in one long marathon bound, to

launch them all at once in order to find their common focus, their mutual centers. Later on they can be edited back and forth as the pieces fall into place, pieces of like color or like tone for each individual Quilt. The pieces are all there; it's just a matter of shuffling and sorting them and then making connections.

The effort of tumbling out all the envelopes I brought with me and unloading snippets onto the cardtable I've set up in my room between the dressing table and the *semainier,* and then shaving off rough edges to smooth each snip, and finally relocating the bits into tidy piles has been a gentle exercise, and has happily proved that the two years spent cutting up magazines at random—waiting for and anticipating the luxury of this time—simply when it pleased me or proved convenient, really has evolved into a workable conceit. Most of the magazine bits relate to architectural details; most are compatibly scaled; many fall within a harmonious color range.

All the tiniest windows and panes I had cut out went into an ice tray. Bigger windows, wall fragments, stairs, moldings, and slices of mesh and grid fell neatly into a small flat straw basket bought at the market for ten francs. Words and phrases snatched from captions or headlines or interesting quotations I hold aside, while random images—a butterfly kimono, birds dressed in evening clothes, cloud shapes and trees, a face or two—spread out on a small lacquered tray.

Fracturing the window bits, splicing them, lining up mullions, rearranging panes according to shape and scale mollifies some sense of voyeurism, I suppose, suited to this place where I sit, behind a window, looking out.

Just last spring I received a postcard from a friend I haven't seen in years who lives very far away—a postcard of a girl severely dressed Amish-style and looking at a nameless land beyond a window. At a distance of time and space, I looked at the card and attempted an answer to my old friend: Who are we now? Where are you? What are you thinking about these days?

And I thought, Where am I? What am I thinking about these days? And looking at my life in a big city, from an apartment and from an office high off the street, am I always holding glass between me and whatever is going on out there?

Is there something I'm missing?

The word-snips float across the table, some cut crisply from their pages with scissors, others torn and jagged so that the strips reveal only partial phrases. Reconstructed into new piles, the words weave and reweave themselves, becoming tangled and disentangled as I move them about. Lacing them to images, words to windows, windows into words, wings me into a trance.

WORD-SNIPS TO REMEMBER

For many artists, a window is much more than an opening to admit light and air

Windows mediate between the inside and outside, provide a transition between foreground and background, and generally help artists focus their vision . . . an opening into the wondrous realm of the imagination

magic places inspire magic houses

FEVER

STAYING

shadows dance upon a wall

Forging

to be very simple, you understand

IMAGES

NOW

AMUSE L'OEIL

I'm interested in illusion. That is what interior design is anyway. How else do you overcome the six planes of the box? One way of de-emph

I feel a need for the slightly edgy, different thing. America is

Cézanne nous a dit de ne pas nous contenter de voir, mais de nous rapprocher de la réalité. Pour celà, il faut d'analyser notre propre manière de regarder

few took the trouble to explore

you're comforted, not forced to make any sort of decisions

VIVRE EN FRANCE

For the traveler, he says, the room is your home, your harbor, your egg

. . . I started to become acclimated to the unchangingness, the gentle relentlessness, and began to sense the deep undertow of an artist's work trance . . .

. . . sitting at a table looking out a small window I . . .

Cicadas signaled the swell of noonday heat and time to reenter this day. Moth and Dad break at noon too, for the mail is usually delivered to our postbox in the village square by noon, and, with it, the newspaper.

Today we were amused by an article on a psychological condition currently prevailing in Florence; described as the "Stendhal syndrome," after the nineteenth-century French author who jotted his impressions of his travels in a journal, the syndrome comprises a series of panic attacks which have struck tourists by the dozens. In fact, the syndrome is taking on epidemic proportions there. People are collapsing before Michelangelo's statue of David, in front of Botticelli's famous painting, the *Primavera,* and in the middle of the ancient Ponte Vecchio. Succumbing to an overload of cultural stimuli, they are withdrawing to their hotel beds, feverish and delirious. They are running out of town in droves.

During our years in Florence we basked in her culture, but we could nibble at museums at our leisure. We never had to chew a city a day as so many tourists now seem to do. In fact, we usually try to root ourselves in a place before setting out to explore "the sights."

The Stendhal syndrome cannot overtake anyone in this valley. The tourist attractions are really few and far between, and take some effort to find. Arles's Roman-built coliseum, St. Trophime Cloister, and Arlaten Folk Museum; Avignon's Papal Palace; the Pont du Gard; a sprinkling of twelfth-century churches, are the biggest draws. Most tourists rush on down to what Pope-Hennessy calls the "bright rind of Provence," the Riviera, which lies two hours beyond us; others fly up to the hill-villages in buses, but are gone by nightfall. The major "sights" are not in this valley at all.

I understand the feeling of overload only too well, though, for that is what I came here to escape. In New York I feel so assaulted by negative stimuli. Here, I sit at my window fingering sympathetically shaded collage bits, and all of that seems so far away.

13 July

Every few days our main mission is to "do Moth's *poste*," a fairly complex task which requires some logistical planning and discussion. Moth writes long elaborately detailed and impassioned letters to her friends. She has corresponded with some of them weekly since childhood. She is one of the few people I know for whom letter-writing is still both an art and an act of faith. When she is here, and I am not, we enjoy a lively and entertaining exchange of letters; not having letters from her from here is something I miss this summer!

Moth devotes a couple of hours each day to her letter-writing, working with a little bin for cards and stationery, a letter opener, address books, photos, flowers from the garden, and a radio tuned in to a classical music station. I am not so studious in my letter-writing this year. I compress impressions onto picture postcards, which speak for themselves, artcards that are wonderfully evocative in their imagery of lavender fields and hill-villages and other native vistas, and I only write letters to Peter at camp—in addition to picture postcards—so that he can share the colorful postage stamps with his friends.

Since I was here last, all of the post offices in our region have been remodeled with new bright-yellow-and-blue metal façades and big

picture windows. From the street they appear cheerful and efficient. Inside, we find the same postal workers as before. The lady up in Ménèrbes will moisten Moth's stamps for her; in Cabrières we lick our own. Gordes has the closest post office, but the postmistress there buckles under the strain of weighing each one of Moth's various letters individually, so we avoid bothering her. Cabrières is handy when we are in a hurry or on the way to the supermarket in L'Isle; Ménèrbes is more convenient if we are making a regular grocery run. Cabrières shares its post office with the local town hall, so it offers a parking lot out front; Ménèrbes has no lot, so we often must improvise, like the French, and pull the Souris right up onto the sliver of a sidewalk out front and cover for each other as we make a dash inside.

Because the locals use the Poste for other business transactions, and not just for mailing letters, we time our visits accordingly. Once a week, on payday, many farmworkers and merchants pay their bills here. The Poste also maintains a telephone booth for those with no telephone at home. Dad places a weekly overseas call to his office from the Poste in Ménèrbes, on a schedule worked out with his assistant there. The telephone billing system is so convoluted, we cannot interpret it, so Michael suggested we call out on his phone only in emergencies to avoid confusion.

Today we opted for the Ménèrbes Poste, and threaded in our daily croissant pickup on the way. We reserve our three croissants and lunch *pain* at the *boulangerie* in Coustellet. Our neighbors, like all the French, patronize specific *boulangeries, épiceries*—grocers—and butchers, and we enjoy the competitive banter: Madame at Cabrières, Peggy asserts, makes the flakiest croissants; no, counters another neighbor, the bread is finer in Goult. We love "our" *boulangerie* in Coustellet and the cheerful mother and daughter, as round and warm themselves as toasted buns, who run it. The croissants await us, hot and ready in a chummy little bag, turned, like ears, at the corners to retain the warmth. Our bag sports a drawing of two birds winging over a tablecloth, coffeepot, and, of course, croissant, and we can smell the buttery scent in our market basket as we drive. Today

Moth bought an olive bread, too, for lunch instead of the standard *pain*. Hard and flat and studded with diced olive bits—including the pit—the bread, pierced with slits, looks like an enlarged lacy mesh or a child's mask gone awry with scissored eye-cuts. For a snack, or *goûter,* I added a sugar-encrusted glazed bun to our hoard, and Moth pounced upon three lemon tarts for dinner.

Driving on to Ménerbes, we swung first into the *"gas"* at Les Beaumettes to reserve the Souris's summer tune-up, and then angled off the N100 and across the valley floor to the southside access to the village. Like most of the hill-villages, Ménerbes can be reached from two or more directions, one typically far steeper and with more hairpin turns than the others. As we wound our way up, we noticed the prosperity of the farms in every direction. Neatly trimmed and tied, vines are already fleshed out with full foliage and clusters of fattening grapes. Some orchards indicate harvests just past—such as the cherries—and others, like plums, appear ready to pluck.

The épicerie in Ménerbes is renowned throughout the valley for its perfect fruits and vegetables because the owner's husband supplies produce to the finer restaurants in the area. We pack our basket full with his recommended selections, and then continue on out of the village to make what Moth calls a little "toot" or backroads spin on one of the tiny arteries that web the valley and connect one village to another. We have found, as we crisscross the valley on our daily rounds, that we can literally choose a different route for every sortie. Some roads are marked on our Michelin #84 map; others are altogether too insignificant to be noted.

Today a loopy detour ran us downvalley, past the left-hand turnoff to "new" Oppède, the lower village of the Oppède pair, and past a gigantic wine cooperative where local farmers can bring their harvested grapes and where they can sell their wine as a consortium. Two rows of enormous cylindrical metal vats, like silos, receive and store the liquid. We have heard that people can come with bottles or demijohn containers or even gasoline tanks to "fill up" on wine, purchased by its alcoholic content—5 percent or 7 percent or 9 percent, or more.

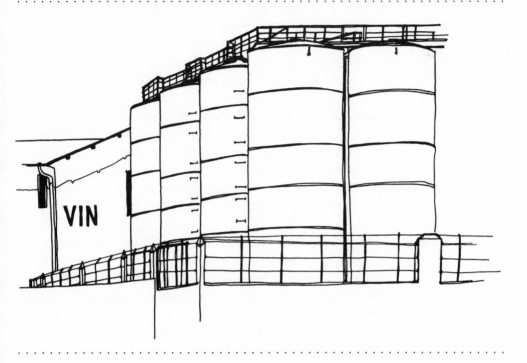

More fields appear to be planted with vines this year. We know the wines of this area—the Côtes du Lubéron and the Côtes du Ventoux—are gaining in popularity as export wines, even to the United States, but we also had heard that a new vine could not be planted without replacing an old root or *pied*. So how many more can be planted?

A number of fields lie fallow, too, on rotation from the vast plantings of sunflowers of two years ago. I miss the grand swaths of gold, but we note the occasional field that jumpstarts and then reverses, green to yellow and green again, as the sunflowers, like sunbathers, rotate their faces to catch the rays.

The wet spring brought an unexpected bonanza of wildflowers to the uncultivated fields and to the sides of the roads. This road we traveled along, not yet shorn by road crews who are blacktopping

throughout the valley, is thickly fringed with sunny clumps of broom and frothy-headed Queen Anne's lace. We noticed an occasional flirt of bright vermilion *coquelicot*—poppy—but it's really past the poppy season now. As chicory only unfurls its delicate, pale blue snaggle-edged petals in the early morning, by the time of our drive it has all shut tight against the heat.

Romans had imported olives to Provence, and the trees we see dotted throughout the valley make us nostalgic for Tuscany—which this region closely resembles. I suppose this is another reason I feel so comfortable here. I remember friends' villas and the same architectural vocabulary, too: ruddy tiled rooftops, and stucco and stone and green louvred shutters closed tightly against the hot Mediterranean sun.

Phrases from Pope-Hennessy's book on Provence resonate on this drive: Provence is for the "amateur of travel—for those who feel a passionate interest in landscapes, towns, atmospheres and human beings." Provence is a "painters' landscape, wholly" redolent with "color memories."

Today Moth and I imagined standing easels in these flower-flecked fields alongside Cézanne, who painted down near Aix-en-Provence, or van Gogh, who made Arles his subject for a couple of years. But not, we argued, not right now, not at this very time of year or day certainly. Now the light is too harsh, too intense, annihilating detail. By midday the views bleach clean of color, and a heat haze suffocates all tone and hue. Color evaporates, and will only return under the golden wand of evening.

At what time of day did these painters immerse themselves in their own saturated color? Early in the day, or late? Spring? Fall? Right now it's too hot, too dry, too brilliant, too bright.

14 July

Today is Quatorze Juillet, Bastille Day, a holiday like our Fourth, celebrating Revolution from excesses of monarchy to lean democracy—or so it was hoped, by both us and them a couple of hundred years ago—and all of France defuses, shutters in to watch the big parade in Paris. This parade, like the May Day Soviet extravaganzas I have seen on the news, exalts the military might of France. Yesterday I moved over to Peggy's to stay in her guest room for the duration of Michael's houseparty, to relinquish my room for his guests from Spain, and so she invited me to watch the parade with her on her television. Installed with coffee and cigarette in a chair by the French door leading to her terrace, Peggy described President Mitterrand's passage along the Champs Elysées. Standing unguarded in an open jeep, he headed the procession from the Arc de Triomphe to the Place de la Concorde, and then removed himself from the jeep and stepped up onto a broad platform where he would continue to stand, at attention and *en plein air*—in the open—for the duration of the parade, a good two and a half hours. I am impressed by his display of reserve, and find it awesome he can maintain his rigorous posture for so long—and even more awesome, in these terrorist days of assassination and bombs, that he can place himself so, without the protection of bulletproof shields. The disciplined screen of the television, of course, frames just what he would have us see, I suppose, and I suppose I may be merely mesmerized by his stance, his public exposure, his austere demeanor and exquisite control. Undoubtedly he has stationed police and secret service to protect him, but to the audience they are invisible.

The Arc de Triomphe, shrouded under a Christo-like crepe of red, white, and blue, loomed like an enormous starched flag at the furthest recess of the television funnel of the Champs Elysées and seemingly endless corps of tanks, jeeps, and firearms. The fighter jets, called Mirages, swooped over the trees lining the Champs, parachuting gaunt shadows into the receptive canopy of leaves. To me, these swift now-you-see-them, now-you-don't shadows, more than any tangible object—more than any tank or jeep or gun—sum up the terror of potential war, and I feel frozen and inept, recoiling into my objection to all violence. Peggy, who has lived close to the political scene in the States and abroad, tried to placate me with the commonly held belief that military might acts as a deterrent, but I've never believed in or trusted such words and I deplore extravagances of weaponry. Today this parade seems more excessive in its own peculiar and horrifying flaunting of gross expenditure than the very wealth the Revolution tried to quell. It seems we have traded one excess for another.

We perceive a military presence even here in our bucolic valley, for every day at this time—and except for today because of Bastille Day—a pair of the same brazen Mirages blasts the sky over our house on regular maneuvers from their base down near Salon-de-Provence. Sometimes they even break the sound barrier and the valley shudders and resounds to sonic boom.

As we drive out of the valley and up into the mountains, we find we must circumnavigate certain areas that are demarcated with warning signs and barbed wire as off limits and are told these protect a cluster of missile sites hidden amongst the most unforgiving furrows in the higher mountains east of Apt.

A friend says that the French give little heed to and care even less about foreigners in their midst; as an American long married to a

Frenchman, she has never encountered the slightest curiosity as to who she is or where she came from. No one really cared, she said; they only knew that she was not one of them. This indigenous reserve goes far towards explaining what we observe here as a tolerance of or lack of concern about these jets and missiles, as well as the absence of interest in the *étrangers* who live or vacation in this valley. Mitterrand himself weekends here from time to time, near Gordes, in a compound hidden behind a high wall, but his presence or absence appears to concern no one but the reconnaissance helicopter which dutifully buzzes the valley when he is in residence. His activities disrupt no rhythm. There are no battalions of reporters laying siege to his comings and goings. No one here wonders what he is doing. When he is here, he is simply on holiday.

This valley and its hill-villages easily assimilate, easily camouflage, easily accommodate. Many residents and visitors alike consider the valley to be a pocket of privacy conducive to discretion and retreat. An American travel writer, wrapping up the valley into a concise pun—hide and chic—remarked only on the values his magazine extols, those of exclusivity and wealth, but, for us, exclusivity and snobbery do not exist. The Vaucluse is, thankfully, no upstart Hamptons-en-France. The disinterest my friend spoke of serves us all well—President Mitterrand, Parisians down for the weekend, and foreigners on holiday alike.

Midday: Moth and I drove downvalley to greet an interior designer, Dick Dumas, who relocated here over twenty years ago. Recently Dick transformed a dreary, run-down roadhouse into a luminescent year-round home. Like most houses here, Dick's presents an impenetrable façade to the road—no windows, no door—but inside his gate, the house opens wide to its view because it is walled entirely in grand expanses of glass. From his living room we can look across a brick-paved patio and sheltered loggia to a crumbling fortress clinging to a nearby, almost adjoining cliff. Dick's vision of his house and this region has always touched us deeply: "It was love at first sight," he says—a love for the "violent drama" of this countryside. From the lush-cushioned banquette in his loggia, the tense and shattered rockslopes fall down and down, away from the crumpled, crusty ruin to the valley floor, indeed dramatic, and we feel as if we are gathered, like pilgrims, in the corner of a gigantic landscape painting, by Courbet, say, awestruck—as they would be—by the coincidence of ruin and rock Dick so comfortably shares with us every summer as soon as we settle in.

But today, Dick had something else to share, a visit with his friend

and neighbor, Lizzie Napoli, a book illustrator who comes down from Paris to summer in a tiny *roulotte,* or gypsy cart, pulled onto a plot of land up the dirt road behind his house. As we advanced up the road and onto the dirt track leading onto Lizzie's land, we caught our first glimpse of the cart through a thick stand of broom. Stationed near a clump of shade trees, the *roulotte* stood out in poster-bright hues: thick bands of celadon and azure wrapped the cart and it was capped with a curved lavender roof; three red steps dropped down from its doorway where Lizzie had hung two curtains, one of beads to fend off insects and another of a bleached toile to pull to for shade. Pale-pink scalloped awnings fluttered at the tiny sidewindows.

The *roulotte* appeared so far removed from the fighter jets of the television as to have materialized here by some magical spell, but Lizzie described it as a purely practical solution to a seemingly insoluble problem. When she purchased this plot of land, she told us, she wanted to build a cottage here as a summer retreat from her Parisian studio, but the village mayor interceded, citing a local greenbelt ordinance forbidding construction. Undeterred, Lizzie sought an alternative. A friend, familiar with her illustrations of gypsies and her appreciation for their nomadic lifestyle, led her to this abandoned *roulotte.* She seized upon it and each summer hires a horse to haul it out from a friend's garage—and here she is.

Laughing at us, tanned and barefoot in a gauzy lavender camisole and iridescent ruffled skirt, Lizzie—obviously comfortable in her role as gypsy—invited us to climb into her *roulotte* to see how everything fits. She constructed a loft bed along the width of the cart at the back, and jigsawed in a workdesk and drawing board and shelves and drawers with the acumen of a master cabinetmaker. To add romance, she festooned the three little windows with snippets of lace and tied up sheaves of dried roses with ribbon which she interlaced into her collection of filmy scarves and necklaces on pegs dotted along the side walls.

With Moth and Dick safely stowed in Lizzie's "living room," a rock-faced pit carpeted with raggy rugs and strewn with lace-covered pillows under a grove of trees, I asked to see Lizzie's illustrations.

She has filled over sixty *cahiers,* or notebooks, with tone poems and spidery drawings describing her perambulations throughout France. Like a gypsy, she wanders as her senses lead her. Her *cahier* on Provence depicts all her favorite villages in sidelong glances.

LIZZIE'S PROVENCE

It is eight o'clock in the morning
and everyone sleeps, still—
except a piano
   sending its letter to Elise
through a window in the pink street
and a tractor
working already amongst the vines
   before day breaks

and at nine o'clock
the mailman's van
will have followed
a trail of gossip
   as it makes it rounds

it was not so long ago
when all awoke
to the tiny footsteps
of a flock of sheep
passing through the village
to graze in the *garrigue*

no one has come
to take the shepherd's place
he died
and the sheeps' pen
loses, little
by little,
its scent

> to take an unknown path
> to enter a village
> redolent with mystery
> to leave one's own name behind
> to see what might be on the
>   other side of the hill . . .
> its profile disappears
> in the heat of the sun
> shimmering, fractured
> like the hum of bees

How does she live here? we ask. The *roulotte* shelters her at night and she draws there when she wishes. During the day this comfortable pillow-softened pit supplies all her basic needs. There is a little spring to tap for water under one tree, and a cooking grill fits tidily into another small stone pit notched into the back wall, with short wooden shelves, also buttressed by stones, holding stacks of enameled tin plates, jelly glasses, jars of biscuits, a bottle of cassis to cut with water from a nearby spring for a cool drink, and cutlery. To bathe, she can visit friends.

—It is not so difficult to live, to be happy, *non?*

Upon our return home, we ran into Michael emerging from his hayloft studio announcing the arrival of his houseparty and, indeed, several unknown automobiles with foreign plates are strewn about the courtyard, edging in on the unsuspecting Souris. Michael, the ebullient host, has toted a leg of lamb and a pot of pea soup—in a tureen, no less—on the airplane from London and cheerfully attacks his menu for the evening, counseling us to retire from the kitchen until he is ready. For the three or four days Michael remains in residence, we creep in and out of the kitchen only when given permission.

At sundown we assembled: a tall, slender, quiet and aristocratic couple from Madrid who are occupying my room; another couple, more effusive, British but living in Brussels, who are ensconced in

Lizzie's Pistou

Cut and dice and mix all together a celery stalk, a pimiento, 2 onions, 2 turnips, 3 tomatoes, 3 carrots, 3 zucchini, ¼ stalk fennel, and a handful of green beans.

Pour a little olive oil into a heavy saucepan and throw in the vegetables all at once, letting them gently brown. Stir occasionally, and, at the same time, heat enough water—4 cups, say—to feed yourself and a friend or two.

When the water is hot, pour it over the vegetables in the saucepan and add salt and pepper to taste, plus two peeled garlic cloves.

Let the soup simmer for about half an hour. In the meantime, crush together one peeled tomato and a peeled garlic clove in a little olive oil, with a branch of basil.

Throw over the cooked soup, and serve—with a bowl of grated Parmesan cheese alongside.

the *oubliette,* and their teenage son who is to work in a vineyard nearby; and a German woman, a filmmaker who will sleep over in Michael's spare room underneath the hayloft. Michael collects people as Moth collects butterflies, as he sprints here and there on his travels. We all know him and none of us do, I expect, because he moves faster than lightning, only settling down to dine or play a few rounds of tennis or attend the opera, which is the excuse for this particular gathering of friends. They all have tickets for Aix and for Orange for this weekend, the height of the opera season. Michael invites us along, as is his custom, but we demur; this is his weekend and these are his friends. We'll happily bump into them as the weekend progresses, at meals or at the pool, but otherwise will keep to ourselves and our routine.

After dinner, Peggy and Dick arrived at Michael's invitation, and Dad complied with Michael's prearranged request: to perform a short cabaret of Broadway show tunes on the piano in Michael's hayloft. Of all music, and even though he is trained in and composes classical music, show tunes remain Dad's favorite. His own father, a ragtime enthusiast, coached Dad early on to the tumbled syncopations of jazz and blues, and from the moment movies went from talkies to musical comedy, he attended every film he could, and especially loved those starring Ginger Rogers and Fred Astaire.

We, too—my sisters and I—were weaned on show tunes and jazz. The very first song I remember learning the words to, when I was about four or so, was Ella Fitzgerald's joyous and bouncing "Goody Goody," and each winter, as soon as Dad felt we were old enough, we drove in from Long Island to see a Broadway show: *Peter Pan, West Side Story, Li'l Abner,* and we loved movie musicals too, *The King and I, South Pacific, Oklahoma, Carousel, Silk Stockings.* Singing them all, we grew up wanting to dance in great sweeping circles like Ginger and Cyd.

I'll even wager I decided on a career in magazines because Kay Thompson sang "Think Pink" to Audrey Hepburn's cinematic *Funny Face.*

In those days, and even now, Dad relaxes best at the piano, letting his fingers frisk the keys, gamboling where they might through his memorybank of tunes, feeling the notes, so familiar to him, sprinkle into his nerves and soothe him. I realize, suddenly and with some surprise, that I hadn't heard him play like this in a casual setting in years, that the tunes and words which I used to take for granted only needed his cue to rush back and embrace me here.

As he played, though, and sang these songs which are more a part of me than the words of any book, I felt an overlay of ambiguity. These songs are so utterly American, so replete with argot and patter and double entendres and in-jokes and references to an America, and especially a New York, of a half-century ago, I wondered if Michael's friends, so polite in their silence, could find their way through the idiosyncratic turns of phrase. We've assumed, arrogantly I suppose, that the flavorful words, the jazzy rhythms and simple, sincere melodies can reach anyone, touch everyone who hears them. But tonight, I am not so sure. We are used to hearing toe-tapping, the gee-whiz laughter that is the usual counterpoint to the sheer fun of these songs; we were not prepared for polite attention. Even through all our years in Florence, when Dad would play at parties around town, and no matter how removed we'd felt then by language, the music always seemed to bring everyone together. Music breached any chasm to communication, and Dad's voice and his fingers, his energy and his rhythms, and his enthusiasm and pure coursing love for the songs always received a generous response in kind—and always laughter.

But not tonight. Nothing happened tonight. Dad played to utter silence.

All at once our very Americanness seemed altogether alien, somehow provincial and isolated from this place and from Michael's guests. Our casual friendliness and banter, our American humor does not ensure easy camaraderie I know, but I had never confronted such a distance as tonight. Dad played, but, quite literally, did not strike a common chord. We were again curiosities, as in Florence, but this time we did not feel at home.

15 July

Today a mistral has been gathering strength, rearing, roiling, roaring, and caroming down into the valley from the northwest. Great hollow foghorn yawns issue from the chimney. Listening to the chimney howl is like listening to a conch shell; the mistral's cries keening against my ear remind me of the ocean. But this wind is dry, not moist, and shears the sky like a blade. There's a brittle edge to this day too, and a seething, malevolent tension is building. I read somewhere that the ozone actually shifts with the mistral and that, after the third day of soughing sound, petty crime supposedly cannot be condemned. It is not the everyday torment of the soul that encourages crime in this instance, it is said, but the madness of mistral.

Mistral days, like today, are cat-nerve days. I feel as if the hair on my skin is being pressed backwards the wrong way on my arms and the back of my neck. *Mistral* derives its name from the Provençal *mestre* or French *maître:* master. I've felt that this day, mastered by the insolent wind, has ushered us all into a dissonant mood.

Outside, our three cypresses claw frantically at the sky—just like van Gogh's in his night sky painting. All of the trees and the bushes dance dervish dances, flinging their limbs and leaves in all directions. Luckily our vegetables, like all fragile plantings throughout the valley, hunch low behind the flexible screens made of dried bamboo

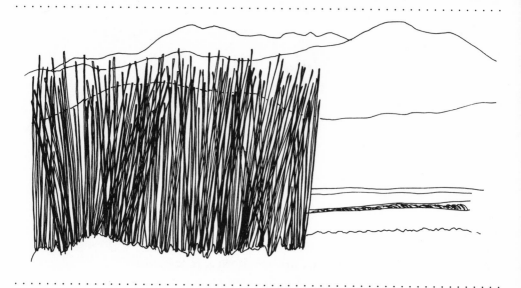

tethered by twists of twine the provençal farmers construct as wind-shields. The farmers align the screens in the open fields so that they will bend with the wind, but never topple or crack.

To counteract mistral, most of the houses in this region proffer windowless northwest façades to the onrushing wind. Only Michael, resisting admonitions to the contrary, made a small opening in his otherwise windowless dovecote bedroom so that he could capture views of sunset, and ensnare nonmistral breezes. He battens down heavy wooden shutters on days like today.

The irony of this day, though, is that we will thank the mistral, for it has broken the humidity and the thickening heat and will leave in its wake air so pure and views so crystalline we'll have to squint, even at dawn, against the unaccustomed brilliance, and we'll have to take sunglasses with us everywhere we go.

———

Today, a Friday, and the Day-after-Bastille-Day, also happens to be a *pont,* or bridge, a day the French leapfrog into a weekend as a holiday bonus. With Michael's houseparty in a flurry deciding what to do and where to go to evade our mistral-tortured terrace, Dad and I abandoned our work schedules and agreed we'd go off on an independent excursion—to explore, despite the wind, and spend a little time together.

Our destination: La Barben, a so-called feudal château in the Bouches-du-Rhône area about an hour distant, down the Autoroute du Soleil. Computerized signs along the open highway cautioned drivers to the continuing *vent violent* as chunks of untamed wind slammed at the shuddering Souris, but off the highway, the mistral's force abated and we proceeded, unmolested, in the direction of the château.

Provence is, in the main, a region devoted to small farms. Châteaux occur infrequently—unlike those in the Loire Valley. In fact, this is only the second self-proclaimed château we have read about in our neighborhood that is open to the public; Moth and I visited the other, the refined eighteenth-century Château de Barbentane, near Avignon, two years ago.

As La Barben, straddling a sheer-faced cliff, came into view, its crenellated towers reminded me of how a solitary monk, bowed over his paintbox, might have rendered the profile of this castle. He would have depicted it, I am sure, in gleaming tints, inserting it, with precision, into the receptive elbow of a gilded initial. Thus the castle would have gracefully introduced a medieval manuscript. In fact, the earliest portion of the château, we were to learn, was indeed constructed as an abbey in that very era. Later additions to the castle were erected during the fourteenth and seventeenth centuries.

Although originally inhabited by monks, the château soon passed into private hands and then, in the fifteenth century, into the properties of Réné of Tarascon, called the Good King and beloved by the Provençaux for his piety, benign temperament, and for his sponsorship of the arts. Réné introduced the muscat grape into Provence, thus securing its agricultural disposition, as well as roses and mulberries.

At that time Provence called herself an independent nation, removed from the jurisdiction of the Crown of France by a self-

imposed authority sustained over the centuries as a result of a close allegiance to the Holy Roman Empire, and then by the territorial imperative established by the Popes who had relocated their papacy to Avignon.

In 1474, Réné sold La Barben into the family who would soon thereafter help force the final union of Provence with France. The château remained in their possession for over five hundred years. La Barben is still privately owned.

During the seventeenth century, La Barben's severe demeanor was moderated by the addition of a curvaceous exterior double staircase spiraling up to the public apartments, and by a specially commissioned *jardin à la française* executed by Le Nôtre, landscape architect to the French court. The interiors, too, ingratiated by less domineering furnishings, were altered to suit a mood of *plaisance,* or pleasure, rather than defense.

Mounting the steep slope to the arched gateway opening into the château's interior courtyard, we could look over a low parapet onto the garden. Calligraphic scrolls of meticulously pruned boxwood curled around tidy beds of ruby begonias. A gently terraced waterfall, coerced into tranquillity by stone steps, trickled through the center of the garden and then tumbled into the woods below. Water, a rarity in this part of Provence, has transformed this retreat into an oasis and even the pines here stand fathoms taller than their counterparts, stunted by aridity, closer to home.

The grandeur of the public rooms open to tourists was mitigated by a casual muddle of the current owners' belongings which included family photographs in plain-jane wooden frames, paperback books and magazines strewn into bins, and trophies from the hunt. All these personal effects breathed life into the otherwise imposing rooms and relieved them of any overbearing responsibility to their history.

A sense of the past, of course, was what brought us to this place, though, and the château was distinguished in its collections of paintings, tapestries, and complement of heraldic shields. The pride of place was reserved for the boudoir commissioned for the comfort of Napoleon's sister, Pauline Borghese, who had visited here. Her jewelbox-size room was furnished with a surprisingly plain *lit de clos,* or built-in bed, hung with cranberry curtains, and a chair. Adjoining it, a tiny dressing room painted in trompe l'oeil as a pavilion or bower, had been constructed ingeniously as an oval to hide closets at its four corners.

Most authentically provençal, to our eyes at least, was the kitchen, its massive stone walls rising almost twenty feet and one wall carved out to create an enormous walk-in fireplace and warming oven. The floor, formed of a miscellany of round boulders and stones from the surrounding woods, had been worn to slippery undulations by centuries of footsteps and we felt as if we were negotiating a rocky shoal as we moved through the room. The robust furnishings were all typical of Provence: a long splay-legged and smooth-topped cherry farmtable surrounded by rush-seated ladder-back chairs of curvilinear silhouette; a fruitwood lattice-faced *panetière,* or breadbox, which had been hung on the wall out of reach of ferreting rodents; heavy hand-hammered copper vessels of all sizes and shapes used for cooking; wine caddies; oil canisters with anteater-snout spigots; and a roughly woven basket filled with lavender stalks because the scent of lavender prevents insects from gathering near the food.

Completing the tour of the château, we decided to chance the restaurant affiliated with the property, La Ferme du Château, located right on the grounds just beyond the periphery of the woods. At the behest of its proprietor, Dad fetched the Souris; apparently thieves are wont to rifle the contents of unattended vehicles and we were counseled to park out front where the Souris could be watched as we ate. Such an attitude might seem to conform to our lock-it-up New York mentality, but we realized, with a start, that we have relinquished such procedures in our village. We leave our front door wide open and the Souris unlocked in the courtyard, with never a thought to break-ins. One of the luxuries of our vacations here, we agree, is the freedom from anxiety for our safety.

It's a freedom, too, which liberates Dad and me here to work fluently. Our boundaries, instead, are conciliatory, those we have come to understand and impose upon our time and our personal goals, our creativity. For boundaries there are; we've talked long and often about limitations, about what we can hope to accomplish within the confines of our own energies and parameters. We work hard—but neither of us is consumed by the incendiary daring needed to transcend boundaries, to fly into the unknown, to achieve greatness. The grand talent, the magnificent obsession, is beyond our capacity.

We work hard. We know discipline. And we lean into the edges of our ideas as into the wind. But in being disciplined—in being neat—are we simply genteel?

As a child, I watched my father track and trail his music, for years skittering over the liquid surface of his desire, not quite settling into it, not quite, really, daring his whole dream, if, indeed, he could look deeply into his whole dream then. A summer of practicing Brahms and Chopin to test his classical inclinations lifted us into our first Mediterranean sabbatical; a few years in the nightclub scene tuning in to jazz reeled us back into New York; and then our Florentine interval when he studied orchestration transformed him into a composer at last and he began to trickle notes and tunes and melodies, both serious and snazzy onto neatly lined paper. And, ultimately, he returned to New York to pursue a flurry of jobs in music administration, and now, his orchestra.

He writes, as I do, in stabs, in time-outs.

Dad is lauded and appreciated for his donation of time and energy, for his altruistic commitment to others' music, but does his devotion to the orchestra become, in a sense, also a shield, a defense, a diversion? Does he hide behind it, too?

A grand obsession requires total selfishness. Is his orchestra—is my magazine, too—a convenient circumlocution, a detour around obsession, an apology for total commitment? Do our jobs, although they provide us our necessary income, steer us away from commitment? Dad's income assures him his summertime; I earned this summer, too, and am glad to be here. But is a summer enough? How much time feels right, or would feel right? How does family fit in? Does family, too, divert us because of compassion and love, or is it also an excuse?

But, I ask, could we have honestly made a total commitment? Where would Moth fit in, or Bill and David and Peter, if we were so possessed? In the context of family, we already take much time for our "stabs." Isn't this enough?

Many artists, it seems, have a low tolerance for the boundaries imposed by family, and some exclude family altogether. Others abuse family and distort their position within that family, assuming authority that forces spouse and children into roles of servitude.

The rhythm and pacing of work, and the need for time and silence: I know these well and I know that I may crudely squelch my child's cry in the middle of a period of concentration, or avert my eye from his intense and needy gaze.

There is guilt that rides on the No's: not now, wait, let me be, I can't right now, tomorrow maybe.

The No's keep me hesitant, at the brink of the edge. Often guilt wins out, and it should; the No's become Yes, and I'll put off my work, put it away until later, much later. I keep a neat desk.

I believe, right now, that I could not sustain personal work either, without my magazine work as counterpoint. I care about the company of associates, just as I care for my family, and I like the symmetry of responsibilities and obligations within that sphere. My boundaries are these. Dad agrees.

Choosing an alternate route for our drive back home so that we could avoid the bombastic mistral, we skirted the southern flank of the Lubéron. The detour brought us, quite by accident, to a hand-written sign announcing the Abbaye de Silvacane just three kilometers, or about a mile and a half, away. Silvacane is one of three Cistercian abbeys renowned in this region; the others are the Abbaye de Senanque, familiar to us and only five miles from our house, and Thoronet which we've never visited because it requires a full day's drive to get there.

The Cistercian monks practiced a strict, austere lifestyle and constructed their abbeys in remote locations at a far remove from worldly influence. Silvacane, set back from the road, hunkers in a low field, shielded from view behind a thick stand of pines which also buffers the abbey from mistral. Its stern façade revealed no concession to ornament and the interior is void of furnishing. A tape recording, though, whispered soft echoes of organ music into the vaulted nave

and a dapper white-bibbed kitten snoozed in a sunny patch on the floor where a thin shaft of light from one tall narrow window created a spot of warmth. In the cloister adjoining the nave, a blowsy and voluptuous growth of lavender, ripe for harvest, lifted our spirits with its tangy fragrance. We felt somehow as cleansed by the stringent scent as by the mistral, and setting our sights upon the brilliance of the late-day sun, we headed home, refreshed.

16 July

Today Moth and I drove Dad to the TGV as he commences a ten-day trip to California to participate in a music festival. Offered a grant for his travel expenses, he makes the journey so that he can hear the world premiere of one of his orchestral pieces, engage himself in a round-table discussion about contemporary music, and he'll even play Irving Berlin songs one evening before an audience. Music is so ephemeral, so tenuous, it does not exist except in the ear, and this opportunity to hear music he had only "heard" in his head and on paper is a welcome reward that even the dread of a fourteen-hour flight cannot inhibit. One of the reasons I timed my sabbatical for these weeks was to keep Moth company during Dad's absence, and to assure him that she would not be lonely while he was away. Still, it seems odd to think of him winging over the Pole so many miles and then returning so many miles—while we simply continue our summer routine.

After depositing him and his little satchel at the curb at the Avignon railway station, we wandered on west, over the Rhône and up past the turnoff to the Pont du Gard so that we could catch the tail of market day in the small "walled city of towers," Uzès.

We avoided the Pont. Even though we have admired the miracle of its engineering and have gawked at its ingenious span of arches which once carried water to parched Nîmes nearby, the Pont has, since our first visit, repulsed me. Not for itself, nor for its construction, which I now enjoy on postcards, but for the crowds of people who climb about on the span—and who have desecrated its environs. When we came here last, to swim and picnic on the little beach below the bridge, we found refuse, garbage, indescribable filth everywhere, and not only paper, but human waste. I have never minded the souvenir stands and food stalls located a respectful distance down the road near the requisite parking lot, because souvenirs and snacks come with the territory, as it were; but it saddened us that visitors, French and foreign alike, could have no respect for this environment, but consider it instead as a public latrine.

So we averted our route. In Uzès, by contrast, we encountered no foreigners. It has always seemed remarkable that the legions of visitors to Provence gravitate towards a few sights while a mere mile or two away beautiful villages or churches or scenic wonders remain virtually ignored. It calms us to wander, anonymous and unimpeded, through villages such as Uzès, shuffling along with the market crowds and doing our errands.

We arrived in Uzès's central Place aux Herbes, where the market is held each Thursday, just as the assembled vendors were beginning to dismantle their stalls. This *place,* ringed by deep sheltering arcades and shaded, too, by rows of luxuriant plane trees, is one of the most beautiful of village squares and feels at once open and welcoming, yet cozy. The harmonious union of stone and foliage is sublime.

We spied the fishmonger rolling today's unsold catch back into his refrigerated *camion* and the vegetableman parked alongside, stacking his display boxes one atop the other in an open van. A few stalls remained alert for one last transaction as the local fire truck pulled in to sluice down the cobblestones. I snagged one vendor who was selling the "hot" summer accessory, a thick black gimp bracelet embroidered with the name-sign of the zodiac; for five francs my "Taureau" will be the ideal souvenir. I like to remember a trip by such small surprises.

Stopping for an ice cream at a bar tucked under one of the arcades,

76

we watched the streetsweepers ply their stick brooms to rid the square of any lingering trash. In contrast to the Pont du Gard, the maintenance of this square and its thorough cleansing inspires both vendors and shoppers to care for and appreciate their surroundings. By the time we were ready to stroll back to the Souris, the square appeared as pristine as if marketday had never occurred.

Returning home, we sidetracked onto a small "D," or district, road, a traditional country road flanked by long rows of plane trees. Lush foliage marked a growth spurt. Plane trees must submit periodically to radical haircuts, and when they are pruned or cut back they appear almost deformed. The pruning prevents them from sprouting up, like home-potted avocado plants, into stringy specimens, and, instead, allows their trunks to thicken and their branches to spread in cathedral arches over the road. Along the most exposed or vulnerable stretches of road, especially those traversing the limestone *garrigues* which endure whiplash mistral, the plane trees to windward cower, stunted to half the height and girth of their counterparts to leeward. And they tilt, too, flinching from the impact of the gross wind.

Many roads throughout Provence, unfortunately, have been stripped of their plane trees as roadcrews "improve" or widen the asphalt roadbeds. Denuding the roads deprives them of their beauty but also of shade; the new, barren blacktops pulsate with heat and in places the new tar melts into sticky pools.

After our D road, we attempted to enter the autoroute to halve

the distance of our drive back, but already vacationers spill south-
ward, like lemmings, towards the Mediterranean resorts. Even at
this point two hours north of the sea, cars were bumper-to-bumper
stalled, so instead we bridged the route and angled south on another
D road through the valley between Bollène and Carpentras. This flat
and arid plain held little appeal: we simply wanted to get home.

Evening: We had reserved seats at the liturgical concert at Silvacane's
Cistercian sister, the Abbaye de Senanque, and so, at sunset, we
hairpinned down through the gorges behind Gordes to claim our
tickets. Senanque, like Silvacane, had been constructed far from
prying eyes and worldly temptation. From the steep descent to the
abbey we could lean over a retaining wall and view the abbey plan
in its entirety. The church connects to an ell of dormitories com-
prising a monastery, and the ell formed by these structures encloses
a field of lavender. The long, blossoming rows, urgent for harvest,
look like furry pinstripes from this bird's eye perspective.

Under the fastidious guidance of a curator, Senanque has been immaculately restored, and encourages tourism through its amply stocked, albeit ecclesiastically inclined, bookstore selling picture guides and music-on-tape, a gallery rather curiously devoted to photographs of the Sahara, and concerts such as this one we were to hear.

Twelve choristers from Russia assembled in the apse of the church. As they sang, the vaulted ceiling of the nave perfectly cupped their voices, note upon note, which then showered upon us like stars. When we came here before, we showed David and Peter how to launch notes into the receptive curve of the ceiling, one and then another and then another, until they formed a stalactite chord of sound. I remember, too, long ago, when my sisters and I would troop friends up into the immense vaulted anteroom of the Fortezza di Bellosguardo, atop the hill behind our house, to sing Bach chorales we had learnt from memory back in school—late, late until the sonority-saturated guards flicked their watches and propelled us home.

Music, this music, Dad's music, jazz music, pop: I cannot imagine living without music. I cannot imagine not being able to sing. I have always envied Dad's ability to play the piano, the way he can just sit down and coax forth any melody he wishes with a quick, facile caress. When I was young my envy or awe was also somehow tinged with caution, though, and, yes, fear, a fear that I would not be able to perform well. I never learned an instrument. I turned instead to pencils and paints. But I still sing.

17 July, Sunday

Over the course of the last week we've noticed posters going up announcing the Gordes festival of the Blessing of the Root—also called the *pied,* or foot—of the Vine, which would feature a 10:30 A.M. *danse folklorique* followed by a provençal mass. Posters multiply throughout the valley as the summer progresses, appearing first sporadically and then more frequently and finally daily on billboards set aside to alert everyone to upcoming local fêtes. July and August spawn dozens of fêtes, many overlapping from village to village, that include fairs and dances, songfests and rock concerts, horse shows and motorcycle rallies, wine tastings and bullfights. The fêtes do not rely on tourism. Instead they provide relief from the hard labor of summer. When I mentioned their tourist potential to Peggy and her daughter, Sarah, both exclaimed: *No!* Absolutely not, these are traditions, created by the farmers and villagers for their own pleasure. If tourists happen to show up, *ça va.*

It's not like the Palio in Siena, then, or the running of the bulls in Pamplona or the Oktoberfest in Munich or any of the once-local, now world-famous events tourism duly suffocates each year. The savvy Provençaux, in fact, have manufactured special long-running events to attract tourists, such as the opera festivals in Aix-en-Provence and in Orange that Michael and his houseparty attended,

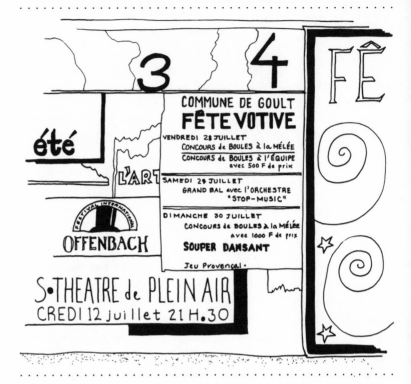

as well as a theater and a film festival in Avignon and a photo festival in Arles, and these more sophisticated, meticulously orchestrated events divert the bulk of the tourists, liberating the Provençaux to entertain themselves at their own intimate local fêtes without intrusion.

The day we arrived on our very first visit here four years ago, we happened to pass an inconspicuous poster at the turnoff on the N100 which announced a circus that same evening in Cabrières, on the *boules* court next to the Poste. As Cabrières is only a few kilometers away from our house, a circus seemed the perfect introduction to our vacation and an opportunity to become absorbed in a totally French fête. We had attended similar one-ring circuses when we lived in Florence and loved them.

Most evening fêtes announce an eight thirty or nine start, the hour of sunset when the skies begin to grow dark, and so, out of habit and believing the bulletin we had read, we hurried through our dinner and drove over with American-bred punctuality. Expecting lines and crowds, we found the tent virtually shuttered and the street empty. Had we misinterpreted the date? Eight thirty came and went, and nine. The tent looked forlorn, limp, neglected in the barren court.

Then, with no announcement, just as we were ready to give up and leave, an elderly woman lifted the flap of the tent calling into the night that the circus would commence soon and to come for tickets. From all directions people straggled, materializing out of nowhere, mothers and fathers and children and dogs, a few from here and a few from there, from doorways and from the bistro and the bar, and a few from cars whizzing into town as if on cue. For ten francs—and half that for David and for Peter—we were handed rough cardboard paddles casually inscribed, in ball-point pen, with numerals. As we passed under the flap into the tent, Grand-mère retrieved our paddles and we all then fanned out over a miscellany of rudely painted benches, chairs, and stools pulled into a casual circle around the sand-filled ring.

A parade led off the show: Père in a black muscle T-shirt. Mère in a flounce. Fille in spangled tights. And Bébé hoisted aloft on Grand-père's shoulder, while Grand-mère, our ticket taker, looked on from her folding chair by the tent flap.

The show: Père juggled, flicked a whip at the horse, hurtled into acrobatic backflips onto a rug, lifted weights. Mère invited the dog onto its hind legs with a biscuit, and danced, and cajoled Fille onto the horse until Fille rode, standing barefoot upon its back, smiling, then flipped and, on her back, juggled large beachballs in the air with her feet. And Bébé was balanced in his father's palm. The crowd of spectators—maybe forty of us, maybe more—hooted *holà* all the while, and at the interval we were offered, for another five francs, candies and souvenirs picked up at the *supermarché*.

And Peggy was correct. This was a fête that would attract no glamour-seeking sightseers. Folks gathered in their workday clothes, farmers in their coveralls, their wives in aprons, and children in shorts or pajamas ready for sleep on mother's lap.

Next day—*poof*—the circus had vanished, sand and all. Where did they go? Did Père turn into a magician and pull his tent back into the hat? Only as our month wore on and we saw new posters begin to go up with increasing frequency did we realize that this circus was making one-night stands in every village in the valley.

Today as we zigzagged from our house in the valley on up to Gordes we stopped at the last turn before entering the village, pulling off onto a blufftop set aside as a scenic overlook. Gordes has been designated one of *les plus beaux villages de France* and from this postcard-exalted vantage point Gordes presents her most dramatic profile. This particular view of the hill-village—a cascade of pale stone houses, the color of new leather, welded to an abrupt cliffside, with the entire valley spread like a quilt beneath and beyond and a castle-fortress at its crest—dominates every brochure, guidebook, and picture book of the High Provence.

But I always feel as I did at the edge of the Grand Canyon: as if the village somehow hovers slightly beyond the reach of my eyes, somewhere way over there, ephemeral and unreal and beyond touch. From here Gordes seems to flatten into a postcard image because it is so very perfectly and exquisitely dramatic. I feel little intimacy with this village; I cannot seem to connect with Gordes as I do with the less frankly picturesque villages such as Goult or Oppède-le-Vieux. Those villages feel more alive to me, more open and revealing, more accessible, and less hungry for tourists besides.

Gordes cleaves to tourism with the most panache of any hill-village—except perhaps Roussillon with its stunning ocher cliffs—and with the most cunning and arrogance. This village senses what will best entice foreigners, but, as a result, has also assumed a cynical attitude, often slighting the unsuspecting tourist with calculated rudeness. The few unpleasantnesses we have experienced during our vacations in this valley have all occurred in this village, and so we do not come here often anymore.

Once summer—specifically August—moves into full swing, tour buses will spew hordes of visitors for a mandatory look-see because Gordes is not only beautiful to see but also hosts a museum in its castle, as well as two restaurants—one good and one terrible—and a tearoom and two ice cream stands and a half-dozen boutiques which cluster nearby. The museum devotes its galleries to the works of Victor Vasarely, painter of prisms and optical illusions; I am not enamoured with his work, and I'd rather see rotating exhibitions here highlighting the work of resident artists of the valley.

Even our honeyman has a shop here now, grandly expanded since I visited last. He has doubled its size and doubled his inventory as well. His boutique sports two new perky scallop-edged awnings.

And in the village square itself, actually a tar-topped V gripping the museum-fortress like tongs, the knitting needles vendor, whose bulb-topped needles are prettily arranged in a small cart rolled to the most auspicious location, now charges five francs to have his photograph taken!

This Sunday, Gordes looked cheerful and inviting, all set up for the wine festival. Jaunty booths joined hip to hip against the comforting haunch of the museum. Done up like little sheds—like our house once looked, but in miniature—the booths displayed casks and kegs, bottles and glasses, corks and winepulls under thatched or canvas roofs. Pride of place matched pride of label, and discussions ensued as to the merits of the various exhibited aging vintages as well as speculations and hopes for the upcoming harvest. Les Vins du Lubéron and Les Vins du Ventoux include robust reds and steely rosés, few whites. A half-dozen sommeliers strode about amongst the gathering crowd; costumed for the mass, they wore flowing green cloaks banded in gold, and floppy green hats resembling truncated chefs' toques. They could have stepped out of a sixteenth-century painting. Their silver tasting cups bobbed against their chests as they sipped their way from booth to booth. Last night, winemakers and sommeliers had joined the villagers in a *grand bal* in the square. The stage, bracketed by gigantic loudspeakers, remained erect next to the tearoom.

Ten thirty passed, then ten forty-five: Moth and I obviously did not learn our lesson from the circus! We could see the folk dancers adjusting their costumes down at the new parking lot at the base of the village near the hairdresser and swimming-pool sales office. Does mass begin on time? No one seemed to mind.

Finally the folk dancers straggled up into the square, interrupting their progress with friendly chatter. At a signal they converged on a flat open area between a line-up of antique Bugattis, which Peter would have loved, and a pizza concession. The costumes emulated traditional dress. Authentic provençal dress, displayed in re-created room settings in the Arlaten Folk Museum in Arles, had been sewn from heavy, quilted plain or patterned wools and linens; by contrast, these costumes are lightweight and made of loose-fitting cottons; for the males, white shirts and brown knickers complemented by black vests, wide red cummerbunds, and black felt flat-top, matador-style hats; and for the females, provençal-patterned skirts and shawls with white blouses and black-laced bodices, and white stockings. White eyelet bonnets set off their faces. All the dancers wore black espadrilles.

Led by a boy about Peter's age trilling on a recorder, and a girl, slightly older, beating a thin long drum shaped like a cucumber slung across her hip in a leather thong, three girls moved counterclockwise amongst us, pressing us back into a respectful circle. They placed the beribboned *pied,* or vine root, in the center of the circle and then, bowing and bobbing heel-to-toe and heel-to-toe, they danced around the root threading themselves in and out pretzel-style under each other's arms. With much bumping into the root and giggling they

coiled us all into a procession. The sommeliers hoisted the root to their shoulders to lead their leisurely way between the wine booths and past the dance platform and tearoom, down a cobbled incline and steps and under an arch into the church where the priests, convened at the altar, awaited them.

The interior of the church, dim and balmy and fogged with incense, was pierced by a single, pane-honed ray of sunlight illuminating what looked like a gigantic provençal scarf. The walls, stenciled blue and white between cranberry-hued columns filigreed with gold, could have been lifted from a dancer's patterned cotton. The half-dome ceiling of the apse, a deeper blue studded with stars, invited an infinity to Heaven.

Provençal patterns have long intrigued me; they seem at once so French and so familiar and yet so foreign. We know the fabrics bearing these patterns, called Souleïado, from the Pierre Deux shops on Madison Avenue and on Bleecker Street in New York. The Souleïado fabrics turn out to be, in fact, not indigenous to this region at all, but were derived from printed cottons imported during the seventeenth century from India. The cottons became so popular, their import and copies threatened the Crown-sponsored manufacture of preferred silks and woolens. The government banned them. At that time Provence still resisted the laws of the central government, and Tarascon, home of the cotton-print producers, continued to manufacture the prints in secret. The ban was only lifted a century later.

In the 1930s, the Demery family of Tarascon counted over forty thousand handblocks—the woodcuts used to print the fabrics—in their warehouse. M. Demery coined the term *Souleïado* to describe the prints: "The moment the sun comes out from behind the clouds to kiss the land," and his fabrics have come to symbolize the sun-dappled richness of Provence more than any other single item produced in the region.

Here as the Mass unfolded we felt kissed by a Souleïado sun. With no pretense to solemnity, words and songs and prayers and blessings unfurled. People wandered in and out, genuflecting, dabbing at the

Holy Water, praying, conversing with neighbors, joining in the chants or choruses of song, or catching up with news—as the mood struck. Help us, they sang, along with the words of the childlike *chansons,* and seek and ye shall find and believe in the Lord and in this root and bring an abundant harvest and good wine.

To us, raised on the strict Protestant gruel of awe and admonition, on the dry wafer and thin, sweetened wine of Communion, this faith, unwavering and encapsulated in the commonplace and in simple song, combines the benign with the inevitable in a way that feels homey and comforting as well as divine.

TWO STORIES OF THE CHURCH

Each year, on Christmas Eve, in Ménèrbes, everyone from the village gathers to witness the traditional *crèche vivante,* or living crèche, the annual reenactment of the Nativity presented by the villagers themselves. Each year the most beautiful child born in Ménèrbes is selected to portray the Baby Jesus and, naturally, the child's mother assumes the role of the Virgin Mary. On this particular Christmas Eve, the infant awoke during the service and, being hungry, began to cry. The young mother, heeding his cry, lifted him from his hay-banked cradle and, unbuttoning her vestment, gave him her breast. Once satisfied he fell back to sleep and rested, content, throughout the duration of the service.

Some years ago, the husband of a friend died in their house in Provence and, upon his death, his widow invited family and close friends to join her in a provençal service to his memory in a church close by her village. At the moment of Communion, the youthful priest asked everyone present to form a circle before the altar rail. Taking in his hands a chunky loaf of whole-grain bread and a flask of local wine, he handed them into the circle. Take, eat for this is My body, he sang as everyone tore a crust from the bread, and take and drink for this is My blood, he added, as everyone sipped from the flask—until the circle was completed and everyone blessed.

Religion here is an extension of everyday life, not a ritual removed from it. This service today integrates into the cycle of land and season, its cautions and cadences and counsel measured within the rhythm of both. I find my own faith resonates strongest in connection with nature—some sort of pantheism, I suppose—and in music, so I feel good being here, listening to this mass with its bustle and hum.

Luncheon: Michael assembled a party of his long-time friends from around the valley to cap off his weekend-long houseparty, a tossed salad of British, French, Belgians, Spanish, and Americans. Chattering in three languages interchangeably and with aplomb, the Europeans exercise their fluency in a manner we find both charming and frustrating. How we wish we had attained fluency in Italian and French! Our forays into French are hesitant and stilted.

Michael's erudite Spanish friend, sitting next to me, encouraged sallies into a mutual French because his English is uncertain and in this language that is foreign to us both we found we could communicate, albeit on an elementary level. He spoke of the similarity of the Catalan tongue to the Provençal, not only in the words of the language itself, but also in fables and songs. Spain lies only four hours distant from Provence; Italy and Switzerland are also close. This proximity of many other nations and other cultures, defined by absolute boundaries, is something we miss in America, because of our country's sheer vast size, even with Canada and Mexico next door. In Europe, with country after country distinguished and distinct by border and language, each holds fast to individual and national pride. In America, even with renewed pride in roots and heritage, the deeper and more intense pride emerges instead from many nations assimilating into one.

I experience assimilation at my very core for I am both indelibly American and mutt, too. From Moth I've come from England and Scotland and France. From Dad, from England, too, and from Germany and the Netherlands. I have a smidge of *Mayflower* somewhere back there as well as a dash of Huguenot, and I can claim a pirate who marauded Caribbean waters. For France, I hold dearly to a thin thread of name: *Bo* for *Bouton,* anglicized to *Boughton.* My name skitters through the thick leather-bound volume, entitled *Boughton,* passed down from my great-grandmother, Melanie Boughton, to my grandfather, Boughton Cobb, and to my uncle. Our particular *Bouton* timeline skips across generations and families, leapfrogging pages and chapters, from its first entry, which is a legend:

> King Clovis, appreciative of certain aid received during the hunt from one of his courtiers, bestowed upon him a singular favor, a button . . .

And thus this name. The word *bouton* also denotes a member of a hunting team, and we like this name hunting us out, alighting upon my grandfather and uncle and nephew as a first name and a cousin and myself as middle names. But much of who I am, or could know about my historical self, is shrouded or lost, splintered, dissolved, sloughed off, like sands slipping back into an ocean of mislaid connections. Our family, sadly, holds to few stories. We tell no tales. Portraits of my father's middle-name ancestors, the Burritts, burned in a warehouse in the Bronx along with most of our belongings during our sojourn in Florence, and my parents shrugged off genealogical curiosity to live in the moment. As we have married and taken on partners and new names, we have blended so well, we recall little of roots. Even my mother, who remembers and keeps in touch with many cousins, singing off their names like a litany, cannot disentangle all the branches of our family tree; and so, it seems, we are close to lost, into our present selves. We are indeed, wholly and completely, American.

Our personal span of American time has rendered us absolutely mutt-pure. We have no particular ancient homestead or land to turn to, nor antiquities, no suits of armor or banners emblazoned with a heraldic shield. Amongst Europeans we cannot link ourselves, as they can, to a village or castle or keep. Amongst Europeans, it seems, despite marriages linking cultures and languages and nations, a precision of identity persists in a way it has not, over time and for many people, in America. We Americans remember family history in decades; Europeans remember theirs by centuries.

We listen to Chouchou and Jean, a French couple who have been restoring a farmhouse nearby. Chouchou, slight and effervescent and of Hungarian extraction, speaks six languages. She feels an affinity with Americans, as she herself lives far away from her native country, and feels now more rooted to their new farmhouse. When new roots, she claims, supplant the old, they can develop more vigorous off-shoots, much like the new roots of the vine which produce new vines, and new and rich wines. Do not minimize your Americanness, even if you cannot trace all your ancestors to their homelands, for your own roots are as firmly planted as ours. In many cases, as we Europeans cross borders and intermarry, we lose connections too. None of us is Adam and Eve!

Evening: A manic drive with Michael in his British Mini took us rocketing across the valley, across the N100, and up into Lacoste, the hill-village best known hereabouts for the sexual appetites and exploits of her most notorious citizen, the Marquis de Sade—and not, as we may have believed, for the polo shirt appliqué! With Michael's guests departed for home, we are just "in three" this evening, and we accepted an invitation to the annual cocktail party sponsored by the American School of Art, based in Cleveland, which holds summer sessions here.

Michael maintains a British automobile—and its appropriately foreign license plates—in France, and, conversely, a French automobile and plates in his native England, to elude traffic violations. This seems sensible in the face of his derring-do as a driver but, of course, it also means that he always drives on the side of the automobile that is opposite the center of the road he navigates and this continually tests his depth perception. This evening a Citroën sideslipped onto the shoulder when its driver observed "no one" at the wheel of the Mini!

Lacoste is one of those hill-villages a neighbor likens to a snail shell, coiling and spiraling tighter and tighter to its summit and the de Sade ruin of a château. The street indeed curls so steeply that we necessarily abandoned the Mini at the base of the village and hauled ourselves on up to the school on foot. In smooth-soled dress shoes, we were tested in our dexterity by this effort, and resorted to picking our way up the smooth gutter trench bisecting the cobbled ascent, using the trench like a goatpath.

Cheerful chatter urged us upward, reinforcing the impression that much of this hill-village has been taken over by the school while it is in session. The school occupies many interconnecting dwellings, on many levels, and each converted to a different study: terraces, in the open air, are devoted to sculpture; cavelike rooms, open just at one end, harbor drawing, printmaking, and painting projects; closed quarters are reserved for sleeping. In fact, we could have shortcutted our ascent through the maze, but we had forgotten the downhill access. Outdoor convocations and school events such as tonight's party are held on a wide shaded terrace, and here we found friends and acquaintances from around the valley catching up on news and moves at this first party of the season. The best-known houses, it seems, change hands—like doing a do-si-do—among friends; Dick Dumas's old house, we learned, has passed through two owners since he moved, and both times to friends of his.

While Moth mingled with the crowd, I asked for a glass of wine in French, only to be answered in undiluted Ohio, and then looked out over the parapet to the view: Whipped clean by mistral, swept free of accustomed haze, the evening blazed in the sunset. Far below the village, the valley flung its luxuriant perfect patchwork, each yellow and green and violet field stitched, as if by silken thread, by glistening road and arboreal filet. Each sunflower shone solo, golden as a blazer button, and the lavender in ruffles, row upon row, inhaled impossibly intense purple into its blossoms. And the bald pate of Mont Ventoux seemed to hover at arm's length, so close it looked as if it were a sleeping giant ready to awaken, rise up, and shed its splendid arid melancholy in the last light.

Just over the drop of the terrace, the ribbed rooftops, anchored by clothesline and telephone wire and television antenna, sprawled in seemingly reckless array. Beyond, on the valley floor, between Lacoste and sister hill-village Bonnieux—familiar to television view-

ers from the miniseries made of Judith Krantz's *Mistral's Daughter*—
little Peugeots and Renaults and Citroëns, reduced to bantam au-
tomata, scooted through the roadweb tugging long skinny shadows
behind them like Zorro capes.

This was the most purely painterly evening; I wish it could have
lasted forever.

18 July

Monday is the day when virtually everything is *tout fermé,* closed after Sunday's gentle debaucheries, and we, too, close in, except to transport Michael to his return flight from Marseilles, the closest airport, an hour's drive down the Autoroute. With Michael and his houseparty packed and gone, we feel quite silent. This is a day to nest again and revert, gratefully, to routine.

What I love most about this vacation and about tending only to my selfish self this summer is capitulating not to a predetermined schedule but instead to my natural rhythm. What freedom to arise when I waken—5:30 A.M., 9 A.M.—and fall asleep when I tire. It does not matter. The sky lightens at 5 A.M. and retains its glow until after ten at night. The day is long, but never feels so. I am not bored at all.

Breakfast	Swim	Letters	Read
Errands	Lunch	Journal	Bed
Collages	Read	Explore	
Exercise	Nap	Dinner	

Or a combination of the above. The easy rituals fall into place, like snips into a collage.

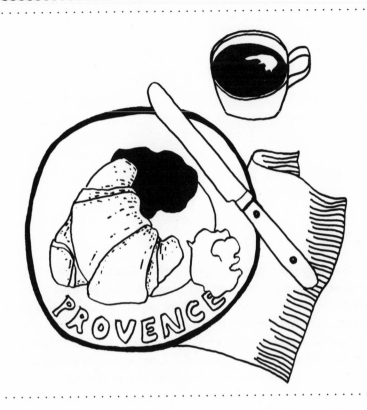

19 July

Today is laundry day and I've finally established my own system for washing and drying, comfortable procedures I pursue between assaults on the collages. Friends back in the States laugh when I describe this Westchester-en-France suburban practice, questioning such plebian activities as unworthy of vacation, but I find the simple rhythms of washing and ironing and hanging clothes out to dry on the line restful, especially in the hug of a genial sun.

We use a small but ardent and efficient German machine to wash the clothes, towels, and sheets. It speaks to us in code, according to load and cloth—from A to J. Then, upon the disgorging of its contents, I iron shirts and skirts and shorts and jumpers while they are still damp. They complete their drying, crisp and wrinkle-free, upon the clothesline. We added new wooden clothespins to the supermarket list last week because they weather and split from year to year. The clothesline had to be tugged taut once again, too, between the tall pine tree supporting one end and the kitchen shutter gripping the other. Philippe tripled the length of the line this summer, slinging another ancillary loop over a thick patch of mint next to the green beans. Our clothes, like dancing sprites, pick up breeze-borne perfumes of mint and lavender and basil and rosemary. We sleep under garden-scented sheets.

Today I followed Michael's example for finishing up the guest sheets. He carries a stack of sheets to the wide landing on the staircase and he then shakes out each sheet over the wrought-iron rail, folding it back upon itself over the rail into long quarters. Then he places each folded sheet, as is, right on the line. The air is so dry and the sun so strong, clothes and folded sheets dry in under an hour—if that.

Evening: We were invited for a drink at Jean and Chouchou's farmhouse in a neighboring hamlet, a long walk, or only-minutes drive, to the west of our house. Over the years their hamlet has remained

a silhouette in the distance, a kind of diorama to our daily excursions. As we have had no tangible excuse, other than curiosity, to penetrate its picturesque veneer, we have enjoyed keeping this hamlet on our periphery, like a beautiful painting.

On this golden-again evening, the hamlet opened to our closer inspection as yet another unpretentious cluster of buildings strung along two roads, one tarred and one dirt. Several of the buildings, connected behind a high wall, attest to the presence of fastidious and well-to-do owners; we can glimpse an impeccably manicured lawn surrounding a lean-lined pool and a half-dozen fabulous and eccentric trees pruned into pinwheeled spirals. Other than that, though, the hamlet compares with ours: It boasts no Poste, no *boulangerie,* no bar. Only a breadbasket resting on a low stoop, and a bucket standing near an ancient well and scoured stone trough used for clotheswashing hint at any communal activity. The effect of the whole is an agreeable if introverted mélange of households.

A hundred yards or so north of town and set back in a tidy field adjoining an orchard and stand of low pines, we found the little farmhouse. The shape of Jean and Chouchou's *mas* is typical of the region: a simple, squat L-shaped building constructed in three stuccoed sections which enclose a living and a dining room and, between them, kitchen and baths. Tall windows, braced by hefty mistral-foil green shutters, admire the Lubéron. A dining terrace canopied with a mat of woven bamboo awaits outdoor meals next to Jean's newly sown and prized lawn.

Inside, Jean showed off a sinuous snail-shell spiral stair leading to the recently renovated second story where they and their two daughters sleep, and an equally curvaceous mantelpiece—both crafted of plaster. We admire the artistry of such details: to fabricate a stair as sculpture to enhance ascent, or to cast a chimneypiece as a caress for fire, not only attest to fine craftsmanship but speak of love as well.

Neither Moth nor I own a country house and on an evening such as this I long for one: We savor the pride Jean and Chouchou share with us. We share their joy.

JEAN AND OUR PLUM TREE

At Michael's Sunday luncheon, we invited Jean to harvest some of the miniature plums in our orchard. Yesterday he came by with his two young daughters, and finding our front door open but us out, he led them through the archway connecting our courtyard with the laundry yard and garden. As he followed the dirt track under our clothesline and through the beans, Jean, in the lead, spied Philippe relaxing, naked, in the swimming pool. *Mon dieu! Hélas!* Oh, dear! Fearing the pure souls of his dear daughters would be blemished by such a sight, he hastily negotiated an alternate route through a bank of lavender and thistles to the orchard. Relief! That afternoon, not realizing that Jean had visited, I too went into the orchard to gather a few plums for dinner, from the thousands that were appended, like Christmas ornaments, to every branch of the little tree. Obviously the presence of Philippe in the pool did not deter Jean from his mission: not a single plum remained on the tree! Jean had taken our invitation literally and had sprung every plum from every branch.

And now, as we depart their farmhouse, Chouchou presents us with a jar of fresh plum conserves.

20 *July*

At 6:30 this morning we were awakened by a *coup de téléphone,* an insistent three-ring clangor that propelled Moth from her bed and down the stairs—and without *pantoufles*! Because we do not use the telephone ourselves, we are shocked by its ring. It was Dad, calling before he retired to his bed last night in California! This crossing over time zones, being simultaneously in one day and the next, unhinges my mental fetters to this day here. I have become so centered on living each moment, moment to moment, in this place, and so reliant on its particular rhythms and cadences that I obliterate the thought that everywhere else holds a time of its own, everywhere else has a night and a day and an afternoon and a dawn and a noon and a dusk, and all concurrent. Bill sleeps while I write this and is at his office, in turn, while I sleep.

Dad's California week differs so from ours. At the music festival, he has attended concerts, given one of his own, has been interviewed about his new composition. He has visited with one of his sisters and met with his music agent and traded news with his office and with Bill over the phone. While here we are, wondering which tomato may ripen soonest and will our honey last another breakfast?

Meanwhile the newspaper speculates, once again, upon the Iran Airbus catastrophe of early summer and will there be a retaliation forty days after, which is when I am due to fly home. There is an editorial on the Democratic political convention taking place in Atlanta. Burma explodes. The ozone layer thins to break-point. Rain forests are felled, never to regenerate. But the chimney swifts are flitting perfect Mirage formations over the rooftop and the magpie flies with its mate and not alone, so we sense good luck along with foreboding. We turn our flower-faces to the sun. Today we will hold tight to this innocent summer as to a life raft.

⊘

At last: We've been invited to dinner at the house I have long associated with Provence, with "Mediterranean," with the essence of good design. It may well be, now that I can finally see it for myself, both more than I expected and less because it harbors the lives and desires of its owners and not simply a dream or fantasy. The invitation jolted a memory-current which pulsed back how many? almost thirty? more? years and exploded in recognition, like a heart's thud on hearing by chance about a long-ago love.

When we lived in Florence, Van Day Truex, a designer affiliated then with Tiffany's in New York, visited us often on shopping trips for the store. On one of his visits, he arrived blazing with discovery: this house, this landscape, these people, this Provence! How he loved his new house! We indulged him his talk, his hands drawing plans for his house in our Florentine air. What would he make of it? How would it become truly his? Smug in our love of Tuscany we easily embraced his for Provence.

And then, perhaps ten years later and by coincidence, one of my first assignments as a design copywriter was to describe this very house from photos taken who knows when because the house had, in fact, already passed on to its current owners. Separated from Tuscany and tethered to my dream of pure design only by a typewriter ribbon in a copywriters' pool, I tried to interpret the house from photos bleached in layout into hazy photogenics. I tried to scan what I could remember of Van's words. What did he say? How could I persuade memory into print, into words which could have been his own?

Van's was a white house, bone white—all white—and sated with sun. Dissolving all surfaces of color, Van distilled design to essences: to sun and space and texture. Whitewashed walls. Palomino stone floors. Blushed clay tile. Straw and sisal. Tawny linen. Bones. Few houses I have seen or written about before or since felt so secure, so right, so comfortable: so Home.

Home is an extension of self, it is said, ego writ large. But so much of what is written about houses does not truly express what is Home. Surface and "style" take precedence over soul and substance. Ironically, Van, although he demonstrated how he bared, quite literally, the soul of his house by simplifying it to essences, and not by capitulating to trend and trendiness, was idolized for his sense of style—and his house was copied over and over. His personal style was emulated by countless designers, and still is. Like perfect pitch in music, perfect sense of design stands apart from the norm; rare and rarified, it emerges all too infrequently.

Style. Appearances. Materialism. Vanities. Michael has Tom Wolfe's *Bonfire of the Vanities* in his studio. I am relieved to be away from Vanities, from Trend and Fashion Statement and Hot Item and Newsflash. I am relieved we have no television—and no merchandised Images in multimillion-dollar picture-perfect packaged 30-second spots. I am relieved to be distant from Hyperreality and Pseudo-Nostalgia, from Instant Heirlooms and Props, the Best and the First and the Finest and the Newest—from the ongoing concern with skirt length.

I feel a loss of home to house.

I sense a loss of design to decor.

In America, design so often dissipates into decor because many people are afraid of scrutiny, and of the self-exposure simplicity imposes. Simplicity demands a commitment to self and to soul. Decor as decoration, sprinting across surfaces, can easily camouflage soul. Decor is theater, and people—chameleon-like—may act any part they wish in their theater and then, when the mood strikes, or whim or temptation or boredom, they can change home and garb to suit the next theater, the next look, the next trend. They can avoid looking into themselves by looking instead only at themselves.

The American Dream has evolved, it seems, to its extreme. The Land of Opportunity has become the Land of Opportunism. Many people came, and come still, to America to shed identity, determined to become someone other than the self left behind. They want the American Dream. They want to live well. The mesmerizing influence of Ralph Lauren and Disneyland point to the twin extremes of the success of the American Dream, a perfectly merchandized Dream. Both imply perfection. The Ralph Lauren style is "perfect." Disneyland is "perfect." Both are theater—both realizations of a New Self, and Home—as buffered from the sad realities of the "real" world.

"Shelter/lifestyle" magazines and their sisters, the "women's service" magazines, which feature home-as-theater and the theatrics of home, base their editorial stance on longing and desire, the same kind of longing and desire that fuels Ralph Lauren's success and the captive crowds at Disneyland. But by implication, longing and desire and the perpetual quest for Dream thrive on insecurity. Discontent generates their energy:

What will They think of me?

What will They think of my home, me magnified?

As the social chasm widens between rich and poor, the lifestyle and women's service magazines, like boxers, face off. The lifestyle magazines, catering to the demographic "haves," preen on luxury and opulence, indulgences and bibelots. The women's service magazines, edited for less-affluent readers, capitalize on quick cures for intimate tragedies, on how a marriage can be saved or a room be RE-decorated or a face RE-made. Nothing is good enough the way it is.

Both are "skin" magazines. Both bank on envy, and envy nourishes advertising. Bloated with merchandise, the magazines cultivate materialism as assiduously as a gardener, pruning a bit here and fertilizing there, and spraying the pests of truth and spirit in the pursuit of the Sale. As materialism consumes the reader and materialistic magazines flourish, discontent swells. Shop Till You Drop, once a chuckle, describes a real addiction, like a drug. And if the readers, many of them also parents, are encouraged to act as addicts, why not their children, too? Taken to the extreme, why not, indeed, take drugs? There's the same hype, the same high, the same "rush," and the same need to consume more.

Where do I fit in all this as an editor at a magazine about home? In limbo, I know, between my soul and my survival, between my ideals and my paycheck. In my role, should I educate or report? How can I reconcile my goal: to show people they can be happy as they are, with what they have, with where they live—when my magazine must "sell product," too? Luckily, for the most part, my magazine honors the way people in the so-called country lifestyle, chosen as our subject, actually live, and I can go into houses and direct photography without manipulating people's belongings and lives. Still, I find few of these houses feel truly comfortable or well designed, as I imagine Van's to have been. Few, to me, are really wonderful.

But then, who am I to judge? I am too critical. Everyone finds comfort in different ways, and I have certainly compromised my own sense of design, though not begrudgingly, to harmonize what I love with the needs of my family.

Why should I impose what I feel is good design upon anyone?

As I travel to direct photography of houses, I encounter "his" chair and "my" kitchen—far more than "our" home. In my own home, we have assumed rhythms that interweave to give us each autonomy within our daily routines. Bill awakens at 5:30 to take his daily jog and then showers and breakfasts, and as he prepares to leave, around seven or so, it's my turn to go through my morning checklist. The newspaper travels, section by section, across the table and then he's off and I awaken Peter to his breakfast and school. David is away now during the school year, but when he is at home, he meshes his pattern to ours. When we return home in the evening, our time and dinner are shared. But I should remember that we each take "our own" place at the table, and I, too, have "my" favorite chair.

How easy is it, really, to create a home that is the sum of two, or more, persons' desires? How easy is it to so tune into your mate that home evolves as the perfect haven for both of your needs and all your mutual, and separate, possessions?

Our house harbors compromises. I have my typewriter and Peter a video monitor for games, Bill his jogging gear. We all have bicycles. David's room is papered in pop-cult posters and Peter's warehouses miniature cars. Our dining room is a workroom and our living room is a television room. Each of us likes some of the things that belong to the others—but not everything. Does our house embrace good design?

I suppose my ideal derives from our last Florentine family home, itself not grand—just a small apartment tucked in a townhouse on a street leading up and out of the city. Our apartment, airy and bright, looked out over rooftops to the Duomo. Whitewalled and sparely furnished, it jumped two levels—where my parents and guests slept and where we all gathered—to a terrace where a ladder led still upward to a roof and to Moth's studio and to the large bare room my sisters and I occupied. Our needs were simple and we found comfort in minimal furnishings: beds, shelves, a table for projects and, for me, for drawing.

We sisters were of college age then, so friends dropping by for a meal and a bath often remained for a week or three, sleeping on the terrace or even between the rooftiles. Moth offered pasta and Dad show tunes. Comfort, to me, consisted of a good meal and good music and a good book and a sunny room—and family. It still does.

Evening: We rang the doorbell of Van's former house promptly at eight. Our hostesses—porcelain-delicate and regal mother, and laughing model-slim, blond-maned recent-graduate daughter—greeted us from a tall window at the top of the house: Come in and straight on up. The door is open. And so it was, quite simply to the street and to their guests. Just inside, their stair—the monumental, refined, pale stone stair from my memory photo of the house as Van's—beckoned us onto its treads, each footfiled to allegro modulations. We hoisted ourselves up three stories, sliding from tread to tread like skaters, grasping a fat coiled rope tied at intervals to thick wrought-iron rings embedded in the wall. At the top, through a small dining room, we arrived at their roof terrace where, incredibly, virtually the whole of the Vaucluse valley dilated to its fullest width and length to eastward, too, on and on, even past Apt. Dramatized by the sheer drop of this house, a vertiginous half-dozen stories down to a graveled garden, the panorama looked as if our hostess had reeled it out just for this occasion.

Instead, she swept aside the view with absolute assurance; she has lived here for over twenty-five years, longer than most of the valley's foreigners, and knows her hold on this panorama is magnificent. When her children were small, she even lived here all year round, trading the winter damp of London for the sharp chill of mistral which freezes soil and stone. Tonight, though, the stones warmed us, like embers, and we sipped on clear peach apéritifs which we held aloft in greeting to each other.

We found ourselves at dinner flung into a cardshuffle of guests, sixteen strong, assembled around two draped tables set with locally made faïence pottery. Again I was reminded of Moth's Florentine gatherings, when friends and acquaintances and drop-ins all coalesced to share our terrace and roof and pasta and wine.

Tonight we floated, as French and English pleasantries sifted, then were dealt out to our allotted places to talk of the valley and upcoming fêtes and art and real estate, for, once again, houses change hands and who knows who will come into town? Among the guests were an elderly retired and seemingly deaf French ambassador (to where, we never learned) and his stately wife in caftan; two young British university students garbed in bohemian black and involved in filmmaking; Jean and Chouchou, included like us because we are all friends of Michael's and "fairly new in town," and a world-renowned conservator of architectural treasures and his mordantly cynical wife. A mixed bag of folk, as Dad would say if he were here.

Dinner, laid out buffet-style in the adjoining kitchen, had been prepared by our hostess. With a pork roast she served onions marinated in a sweet wine, thick tomato slices drizzled with vinaigrette, *haricots verts* as slender as pins, and, to start, a warm zucchini tart crested *au gratin*.

Descending two levels to the living room for coffee, we dispersed amongst the assorted sofas, ottomans, and benches surrounding an enormous low table piled high with art books—here again the *Vanities,* seemingly the house gift of the season.

Here the image of Van's design faded. The room is thoroughly and preciously decorated. Our absent host, an antiques dealer, displays his trade in his deft maneuvering of objects, but the room seemed rather too crowded to my eye, too full of treasures and collections and books. I look for structure, for bones, like the remarkable stair; I feel no need here, remembering Van, to be seduced by decor, no matter how well bred.

As I gazed, the amiable bubble of chat was suddenly pierced by a low ominous drone. A *freulon*. Immense and black, this species of wasp is so deadly that firemen must, by law, be summoned upon discovery of a nest and the police carry serum with them to counteract its lethal sting.

The men, rallying as a team, leapt upon the sofa cushions and brandished aerosol cans of insecticide to quell the pest. The insect slowly, heavily, and oh-so-insolently circled, then finally fell, and was trounced by Jean's heel. Suddenly this brief duel, this momentary dance with death, made the room feel cozy, and beautifully, appropriately intimate. Turning back to the guests, I relinquished Van's memory-photo for this one, of a dinner party's small victory, and when conversation reasserted itself, in a tone of calm relief, we found it a good time to say good night.

21 *July*

I have always loved faïence, the fresh and unpretentious glazed provincial earthenwares typically associated with the Mediterranean, and especially with Provence. Illustrated with naïf figures or flowers or birds and slip-trailed with sinuous thin bands of color scrolling along their borders, these are modest wares, homely, suited to a casual environment. In New York our kitchen shelves hoard a set or two of Moustiers, named for the village in the mountains southeast of Apt where it is made and which Bill and I received as a wedding present eighteen years ago. Our larger set is populated by cheerful farmers turned out in smock, pantaloons, and hose gamboling amongst daisylike blooms—and this pattern is still produced today. To visit Moustiers, however, would require an overnight stay neither Moth nor I cares to make, so Moth planned an alternate outing up north into the Drôme to Dieulefit where the pottery commissioned by the Souleïado shops is made.

On an earlier visit with a friend, Moth had reviewed stacks of a then-trendy design: whitewares dappled with clusters of pastel pindots. If Dieulefit's potteries only respond to and display what is chic we'll undoubtedly find this year's hit, octagonal dishes dipped in intense monochromatic glaze—red or russet or ocher or blue or teal or black—and goosebumped along their rims with pearls of like-colored clay.

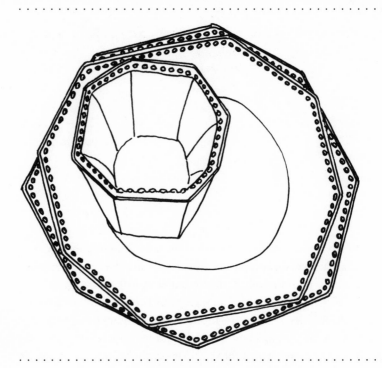

On no visit have I exited Provence, except to tour some Roman ruins northwest of Mont Ventoux, and I noticed as we drove that the landscape here changes markedly, to the more emphatic dromedary foothills which lead on and over to the higher Alps. More aggressively scaled than our ridges and gorges, and more compressed, these mountains sprout thicker and darker stands of pines and, instead of *mas*-style farmhouses, we noticed more *bastides*—stocky, turreted, fortress-like dwellings—which had, indeed, once served as both defense and as habitation. Fields were adroitly insinuated into the wild, collected like handkerchiefs in pocket furrows or sprawled over terraces ingeniously notched into embankments along our serpentine route.

Although Dieulefit lies off the beaten track, it has achieved a reputation as a mecca for bargain hunters who are cognizant of the continual *occasions,* or sales, the potteries hold to unload stashes of seconds and overruns. All the shops along the main street through town were clogged; Moth remembered the *poterie* she had visited as being beyond town so she hastened the Souris straight on through and out the other side and on until, *le voilà,* she announced a low-slung warehouse set back from the road.

Like the shops, the warehouse contained a cache of overruns and our hunch was correct—everything matched up with this summer's Souleïado wares. Stacked, piled, spilled along crude floor-to-ceiling shelves, thousands of plates and bowls and pitchers and ashtrays filled the cavernous warehouse, and all with the goosebumped pattern. In one corner was a box of miniatures, almost like old-time salesman's samples, of variously shaped dishes, and I bought a few of these for about five or so francs apiece as small mementoes and for gifts.

I had hoped, though, also to observe the pottery being formed and molded, coddled and caressed, and heated in the kiln. I love seeing how things are made; I've watched artists paint fine porcelain in Copenhagen. I have observed glass blown outside Venice and tried my own hand at the craft near Helsinki. And looked in on Maseratis assembled near Mantua, stereo headsets tuned up in Milwaukee, tins pressed into muffiny-form in Chillicothe, and tartan woven on a kilt-wide loom in Scotland.

So, feeling suddenly insolent and impatient at missing out on what I had expected to see, I stamped out to the car—and into a splintering migraine. A crocodile-crackled aura began to fill my field of vision, steadily and inexorably, until the jellied ocean inside my eyes flared to throbbing yellow. A pulsating question-mark of blindness inched across, arcing upward and outward from right to left, and as I tensed to the inevitable pain I grew angry too at Moth, because, having driven me here, she professed disinterest in the pottery and sat, waiting, in the heat in the Souris, while I was inside. Why did she come if she were reluctant to share this experience with me? Why did I suddenly feel such guilt?

Although we live in the same city and telephone each other regularly, we have not spent any continuous time together in over twenty years. For years, too, I shrank from her, years when she slouched into alcoholism, years when she was maudlin and difficult to handle. Although fully recovered now, she can still trigger, even after fifteen years of being well, and with the slightest word, my tortuously constructed chrysalis of tolerance with remembered pain. She finds it awkward to slow down with my sisters and me; almost as if by ingenuously glossing over conversation with quick doses of cheerfulness, she will slide over or fill gaps she dare not penetrate with intimacy. In the aftermath of her illness, my sisters and I still cringe from intimate contact, with anyone, touching only hesitantly and briefly and ever so cautiously as if our skin would burn.

After the pain, Moth is cautious with us, sometimes afraid of us even, as we are, in turn, still tentative with, sometimes afraid even, of her. And yet she has many friends, dear friends and close friends, friends with whom she can allow herself to dare, to be expressive in a way she cannot with us. It is easier for her to be a friend. Perhaps we hurt her more deeply.

It has never been easy for her to be a mother, either, for she was still a child herself, really, when we were born, and untutored in childrearing. Alone and inexperienced during the war years, she left much of our care to a series of nurses or sitters, and only when we moved to Florence did she turn and really see us, and begin to find out that we were three and not one, that we were individuals and not just "the girls." When we were young, we were always "the girls," always dressed alike, our hair pigtailed the same, and we were sent to the same school. Occasionally, we would shock her with a bout of single-mindedness, and occasionally, tellingly, an accident or illness. I broke my arm, Wendy cracked a tooth, Candy passed along the mumps. But it was easier in the long run to passively fall back into the mold of "being sisters" and alike.

During all those years it was not easy for her to be a daughter either, as her mother, our grandmother, lived in a self-imposed state of perpetual and presumed illness. She wielded a terrible authority from her bed. My grandfather, and my father, learned to deal with their women by pursuing autonomous interests, my grandfather botany and my father music. My mother's brother, quiet and aloof, kept a sailboat and a seaplane; he, quite literally, could fly away. Although they were always physically present, we sisters sensed that the true thoughts and dreams of these men were held just out of the women's reach, elsewhere. These men were, to us, untouchable, and in being so, we dearly wanted to touch them and what they did. We listened to music and we sang; Candy grew proficient at the guitar. We collected ferns, my grandfather's specialty, and pressed them into albums. We watched him as he nurtured butterflies in their cocoons and then, when they emerged, we helped him set them free. And I sailed with my uncle whenever I could, and flew with him over the ocean in his sea-plane when the winds were still.

The risk of family is, of course, a risk of blood, a risk of life and death. Like all children, we believed our parents perfect, and if they were not, we would surely die. So when we moved to Florence and grew to know each other, parents to daughters and daughters to parents, for the first time, we reveled in a new intimacy—until, horribly, my mother fell ill, and my father withdrew into his alien-to-us world of music and friendships we could not presume to enter.

Between friends, imposed distance need not threaten the relation-ship. Within family, imposed distance can be construed as hurtful even in its honest attempt to prevent hurt. Or distance can be used as a weapon, or to avoid touch. Throughout my mother's alcoholism and beyond, Candy, through the convenience of her marriage, has always lived far away. Wendy lives at a remove as well.

My distance is imposed by work and other obligations. Moth and I do well by correspondence; we exchange wonderful letters and we converse fluently over the phone. When we are together we are cozy but still careful of each other and in subtle ways test the bounds of what we can dare. Our reactions to each other and our defenses are reinforced by the code of ethics, or etiquette, we were taught by family: never show your emotions, keep to yourself, anger must be avoided, never raise your voice.

And so here I react—overreact, and harshly—to her, unconsciously reviving some ancient defense to her old and blurry days. I criticize what I see as a heedless approach to experience—to mask an event in anticipation, in planning, and in remembrance. Moth will often hurry through an actual outing, pressuring it into memory even as it is unfolding. She will drive anywhere at the merest hint, but does not care to linger.

Moth is a quick study. Her eye is acute as is her ear; she picks up texture and timbre in an instant, and she remembers whatever she observes in precise detail. Her eye is needle-sharp, too, plunging into the core of whatever she observes or wants to see. Not surprisingly, she had studied photography in college and was a fine practitioner in the art of portraiture. Snaring her subject, she distilled what she saw to an essential and uncluttered image: She framed her subject cleanly, right to the edges of her film—and yet her edges and the edges of the film never once confined what she saw. She worked with an old Rolleiflex, and when she shot twelve images, she achieved twelve images. Some of her photographs hang in her stairwell: an Egyptian pausing at prayer in a shaft of sunlight in a Cairo mosque; another guiding a skiff on the Nile . . . and there are two portraits, of my father and of her brother as teenagers, gazing into cloudless skies and into their future.

Perhaps because she imprints so readily, she feels free to move on quickly, to her next image. I must graze more slowly, and I only remember shards, impressions, slivers, and rarely everything of an entire experience. I must constantly coddle my sense of recall with snapshots and notebooks and journals and postcards, while she re-members everything without cues.

And so, I have to let go of my criticism and my defense. I must remember that she has her own way of living through her day, as I have mine. I have to remember that we do not have to synchronize. When we came to Provence four years ago, Bill and the boys and I, we all tripped over each other, stumbling into unexpected abrasions: when to eat, who will cook, what about laundry. I was unaware that Moth dislikes dining with children, but she wouldn't immediately admit to it, couching her feelings in cautionary digressions such as "the children won't want to eat as late as we do" or "they won't like what we are having for dinner." But, then, she didn't know then that I hate to cook, but don't mind chopping and slicing and gathering ingredients, and I don't mind washing up. She had assumed some sort of territorial control then, too, dispensing rooms and corners to us out of the way of her letter-writing and Dad's musical scores. We had to machete our way through a thicket of asides to arrive at a discussion of turf—and terms. After all, we were paying half the rent. It worked out at last, but I found myself constantly vacillating between being obedient and asserting myself.

As I am today. I am finding it difficult again to slip free of the "be a good girl" noose. Because in some recess of my soul I know I returned here this summer to be a daughter again, a daughter that could be protected and sheltered from the world somehow and a daughter that could take for granted perfect parents.

Because it feels so good to write and draw and read and make music and enjoy this place, I guess I expected our rhythms to intersect in some idealized harmony of projects and diversion. If I am to be a daughter again, shouldn't our rhythms mesh?

No, say it again: We are not the same.

So, when the actual pain of migraine hits, I look at her and she at me and we decide to stop exploring and go earlier than planned to our lunch, to simply make a space in this day for nothing more than a leisurely and luxurious meal, without much chat, without expectations, without commitment to anything but a quiet time. Moth is relieved. I am too. I realize, of a sudden, that she had suggested this daytrip as a gift to me, and this migraine, which I resented as sabotage, was instead a message—to give myself to this lovely day, and to her company.

Retracing our route, we wriggled the Souris back down through the mountains, turning off at Le Poët Laval, another of the villages singled out in the *Inventory of Historic Monuments of France*. Protected by toothy ramparts, the village clings, Velcro-like, to its mountainside. We edged our way up to the top of the village and then walked partway back down along a cobbled track to our destination, a small and discreet guidebook-starred inn and restaurant called Les Hospitaliers. Occupying several contiguous houses and enchanted by an abandoned twelfth-century chapel and tower ruin, the inn attracts a genteel clientele. Each of the twenty or so suites, unobtrusively built into the side of a hill, opens to a mountain view, but to visitors to the dining terrace, is invisible. Stepping through the entry gate, we came directly onto the terrace without passing through any of the public spaces shared by guests. Leaning over the wall of the terrace, we could see a neat, mosaic-lined swimming pool sheltered amongst cypresses and pines and a small lawn, a sweet retreat for tanning and a nap. From the terrace, too, the mountain ranges receded, rank upon gray rank, into a gauzy infinity worthy of an art card.

We settled ourselves in a shady corner at a table decked in linen of a sunflower hue, and under a wide-spoked orange umbrella scalloped to thick fringes. We selected the *menu fixe,* a treat and an indulgence for us at 170 francs, or about 28 dollars. We rarely eat out like this, and we decided to sample the specialties of the restaurant and of these mountains. To start we were presented a delicate cream of haddock soup warmed under a plump pastry bonnet which released a swift soft *woosh* of steam when punctured with a spoon. Guinea hen, or *pintade,* trapped locally, followed, sliced wafer-thin and arranged in a fan in a raspberry-tinged sauce.

Suddenly, a capricious flutter of mistral lifted our umbrella and tumbled it around the terrace like a top. A restless toddler, in striped sunsuit and tiny jellies, wobbled under its circus-flap fringes, only to be scooped up by the waiter and carried off like a cherubic trophy to say hello to the chef. *Pouf!* The wind subsided as quickly as it came, the toddler returned grinning with a biscuit, and we too relaxed into a compatible calm, settling into a cool and deliciously tangy sorbet and the drowsy afternoon.

22 July

I have finished a novel set in France, written by an American author long affiliated with the *The New Yorker,* William Maxwell. Entitled *The Château,* the novel follows a youthful well-to-do American couple on an extended holiday in Normandy and Paris just after World War II. They reside for a time as paying guests in a chilly château and are captivated by and captive to their naïve expectations and preconceptions: How will they be received as guests? Can they become friends with their hosts? What is their position within the web of etiquette in the lives of the people they meet?

The curiosity of the book lies less in its revelations than in its cadences, which reveal more than facts. The book unfolds as if a Frenchman were observing these Americans in their efforts to, in turn, understand the French. Turns of phrase, idioms, specific words standing apart recline in the ear as if someone French and not Illinois-born were uttering them.

"There is nothing so characteristic of a civilization than its manner of speech," wrote British author and travel writer Freda White. In her discussion of language, she qualifies French as "clear and definite" and English as "flexible and vague." Discussing her own efforts to translate French into English, she rationalizes her methodology: to render French as the French themselves would, into a strict and formal code. Reprimanded by her critics for sounding "stilted," she felt, in fact, that she was privileged to translate more than words, but also a specific and appropriate cultural attitude towards language as well.

Words taste in the mouth like foods, and are just as culturally distinct. Words may be munched or swallowed, chewed or swirled like wine, or inhaled or even expectorated in little gasps of spittle. French to me seems piquant, like her cuisine's sauces, with words, like spices, distinctly balanced within the recipe. Italian flows from the end of the tongue, like spaghetti, and like gelato, slides tart behind the teeth, and yet smooth. The Germans package their syllables, in bombastic bursts, like sausages into their casings. And in America we've gone all slurry, it seems, mushed into a fast-food of slang and acronyms, epithets and rap which jiggle our language around; we serve up our words in a rush.

I have heard that there are literally dozens of words in Eskimo or Inuit for snow, words describing every nuance of flake and white and wind. My thesaurus skitters through word thickets, too, piling them into cozy mounds which I pick at every now and then to escape redundancy.

Words are my music. I listen to books, like *The Château,* energized by their vibrancy. In college I had a friend who always weighed her words with consideration and restraint; I view authors like Maxwell much as I remember my friend, as a caretaker of language. I relish their words.

Reading *The Château* and conversing with Europeans makes me wish for a balletic turn of tongue. It would serve Americans well to be required to learn two or three languages, if not more. Much can be lost in translation, if the translation—unlike Maxwell's or Freda White's—does not incorporate nuance and attitude, argot and slips of tongue, pauses and lapses, and incongruities into its prose.

Today, Leah, who is an interpreter and translator, came to visit; she gives Moth a lesson in French each week to help her jump the hurdles of everyday transactions and errands. This morning Leah rolled off into a long discourse on "culture," bewildering us completely because she returned again and again to tomatoes and lettuce. We had misinterpreted culture to mean art and music; Leah was, instead, discussing hydroponics, or cultivation!

EXTRAPOLATIONS

In English	*In French*
canapé, as cocktail nibble	*canapé,* as sofa
traitor, as betrayer	*traiteur,* as caterer
factor, as element	*facteur,* as mailman
etiquette, as manners	*étiquette,* as label
frequent, as habitual	*fréquent,* as steady boyfriend
occasion, as event	*occasion,* as final sale

And Americanisms

Le picnic
Le weekend
Le parking
Le pressing

Midday: We enjoyed one of those extended indolent lunches with a friend of Moth's, partaking of robust simple foods and talk of family and mutual friends. Just around the snout of the Lubéron, Moth's friend Bannie, who is spending three weeks here to write an art paper on a nearby cloister, has taken a *bastide* planted on a platform in a tuck in the mountainside. The *bastide* has sturdy towers at its four corners and a corroded stucco façade punctuated by long green lou-vred shutters folded at the knee against the intense sun. A wrought-iron cross atop its arched gateway leading to a courtyard signals that this particular *bastide* was once a rest stop on the road to once-papal Avignon.

Bannie's landlord purchased their *bastide* from the farmer next

door; their property is just a slot indented into the broader farm, and so Bannie is awakened each morning by the farm tractor revving up in its shed right beneath her bedroom window—on land that is not parcel to this property at all. The flexible solutions to buy/sell or to rent intrigue us. Some people downvalley from our village bought a *mas* they cannot inhabit or even visit until its owners die; others sold rights to their village townhouse, to go into effect after their death so that they can avoid taxes now; still another sold with the stipulation that he can always spend his August vacation in his house—with his furniture intact.

So the owners of this *bastide* shoulder their neighbors without an inch to spare and can only hope the land surrounding them will remain undeveloped.

Although the exterior of the *bastide* has been unaltered, the white-washed interiors, both upstairs and down, have been scooped clean of any ornamentation. Furnishings fulfill basic needs; a few slouchy cushioned rattan chairs encircling a round table; a secretary; armoires; beds; a hutch.

Bannie set out her buffet in the kitchen and then we lolled around the table long into the afternoon. Glossy black olives pungent with brine and slicked with oil, chewy thinly sliced prosciutto and crusty chunks of whole-grain bread from the farm, mounds of crunchy celeryroot, tomatoes to gnaw and slurp like peaches, chèvre, and strawberries with *crème fraîche*—as long as the olives lasted, why go home? Why not, instead, enjoy thin blades of sun slicing tile and rattan, listen to the lazy burr of beesong against the windowglass, and sniff the gentle hint of basil potted by the door?

23 July

W̲hen we go forth on our exploratory tours of the countryside, we always know when we have returned to the embrace of our neighborhood because the Commune of Gordes adheres to a strict building code requiring that, for the sake of uniformity, all houses be faced with the local stone, a powdery golden limestone that flakes into fat pancakes and stacks easily to make crusty drywall. Peggy reminds us that the new code actually promotes and protects an illusion of uniformity—that prior to its enactment, the houses were always sheathed in thick coats of stucco and only the sheds and dependencies and outbuildings had been constructed of drywall. The rigid adherence to the drywall look she finds rather an affectation, but I like the pale and brittle gold of the stone and the precision of the placement of the stones. Some early buildings had been built with the stones laid so precisely, in fact, one can understand the lack of mortar; these days, a cementlike mortar is used to bond the "dry" wall on all the new houses.

Drywall distinguishes retaining walls and property dividers throughout the region too, with the flat stones upended along the top of each wall much like barbed wire might be back in the States.

The most inspired and mysterious examples of the drywall construction are exhibited in a little museum village of primitive conical hutlike dwellings called Les Bories just a few kilometers from our house. The word *borie* means "cavity" and these curious buildings appear to be just that. *Bories* dot the landscape throughout the valley; this village clusters a group of them into a hamlet. Some of the *bories* have wooden lofts constructed inside for sleeping; many have bake ovens built into a little wing extending from the central "hall"; and shelves are simply fatter stones protruding into the room. Smoke from interior hearth-pits has charred the stones inside many *bories,* despite ventilation holes built into the conical roofs. Doors may be of more recent construction and are very heavy and made of wood, while windows are simply vacancies left between the stones.

No one really knows why the *bories* were built nor how old they might be. Meticulous and scientific methods of dating stone establish them as "younger" than they appear, perhaps only a couple of centuries old at most, and not the prehistoric dwellings they were long presumed to be. Over the years shepherds often used them for sleeping or for storage, and it is said that they were used as hideouts during the Résistance. Today they stand in silent testimony to a unique method of building and that is all.

It is lucky that Michael and Peggy and their neighbors bought up their protective greenbelt for orchard, vineyard, and lavender field, because new drywall-sheathed houses are popping up on every ridge between the N100 and Gordes. A mere ten or fifteen years ago, Peggy's daughter Sarah could ride her horse from their house straight on up to Gordes—a distance of about seven kilometers—stopping for a sip of wine with a farmer or two she knew along the way; now she would be inhibited by so many houses she would have to detour onto the main road.

Though quite a few houses appear to be under construction this summer, I don't feel as bothered by the development here as I do back in the States. There, developers peel back topsoils like plastic surgeons exfoliating skin, and yank out trees like orthodontists pulling teeth. Oblivious or insensitive to the natural contour of the landscape, they level, scour, and bare their parcels of land for Parades of Homes where different builders can exhibit their wares as if on a shelf. Like computer print-outs, neo-Tudor, neo-farmhouse, neo-Victorian, neo-château, and neo-Cape houses scroll out along the Parade. Only the façade tells which is which. Inside, the floor plans prove virtually identical: living room, family room—one or both with a fireplace—eat-in kitchen, usually enhanced by a breakfast nook, master suite with twin vanities and, these days, whirlpool bath, walk-in closet. The consumer shops for a style like a jar of mayonnaise or box of cereal, and the builder will reproduce the chosen dwelling following its prescribed plan, and simply affix the façade the consumer fancies most. After this sabbatical I will return to just such a project, to decorate it for the magazine. As I write this, the house is being erected on a featureless patch of denuded terrain, plugged in between two just as hastily constructed houses. It will be presented as a Cape-to-copy for our readers and its façade will emulate its Massachusetts forebears; turn the corner, though, and sides and back will be blank, bereft of detail.

In America, façade is what sells. In construction, corners can be cut, and often are, and oftentimes inferior materials are used to save on time and money. Here, it appears as if builders still practice time-honored techniques. Many of the houses are constructed of low-cost concrete block—because there is no timber available—before receiving their stone facing, but there seems to be an attention to detail I find lacking so often in new American construction. Perhaps Sarah, used to studying the architecture of this region, would disagree—and relative to ancient construction where every stone mattered, she would be correct—but relative to much of the shoddy construction evident in American subdivisions, the building here seems to respect inhabitant and landscape.

The Gordes code also imposes severe restrictions on historic dwellings and hamlets such as ours. None of the buildings facing our village square can be altered, and so Sarah cannot add windows to her little cabin nor can Michael place a window in Philippe's windowless tower bedroom.

In the evening, though, Moth and I were invited to dinner in a small hamlet—smaller than ours—that was not inhibited by an "historic" appellation, and thus its owners were permitted to convert the complex into a family compound. Curious to observe what could be achieved within the general confine of code, I asked to tour the complex. What they have done, in sum, is to create a village in microcosm and impeccably—perhaps even too perfectly—to stylize the basic architectural elements of their clustered structures to serve their own particular and specific needs. As a retired couple, they wanted a holiday retreat for themselves where they spend an extended summer vacation, but they gracefully incorporated separate dwellings for children and grandchildren into the set-up as well. The buildings neatly tuck one into the next, just as in our complex, and so we were unaware of where one family unit ended and the next began. In fact, we were surprised to learn that each unit could open a door to a mutual patio and thus the families could congregate when they wished.

The craftsmanship of the complex ingeniously married antique architectural elements with modern amenities; provençal details such as a cistern, groin vaults, and Romanesque-style arches were restored but did not inhibit the insertion of contemporary necessities such as kitchen appliances, bathroom fittings, and storage which were all skillfully fused into the architectural surround.

It was hard to imagine that what they had inherited when they had purchased the complex a few years ago was a dismal ruin, but as the Gordes code requires that all exterior renovation be completed within two years, they had to harness all their reserves to meet the deadline. Every stone had to be reset—but this time with mortar to ensure durability. Now they have relaxed a bit and are tackling the remaining interior rooms one by one.

Dad has been invited to play and sing a Cole Porter medley here in a couple of weeks, and we saw where the piano would be set up and where guests would sit. Sliding glass doors roll into pockets in the dining room walls, creating an intimate cabaret-like setting, and the terraced patio will hold a dozen or so tables, each with perfect sightlines to the "stage." How beautiful it should be, with trees strung with lights and the Lubéron behind!

24 July, Sunday

Depending upon our household needs—or upon mood—we circulate through or tactically avoid the weekly markets which rotate from town to town throughout the region. We are familiar with the schedule:

Monday: Cavaillon
Tuesday: Gordes
Wednesday: St.-Rémy
Thursday: Uzès
Friday: Carpentras
Saturday: Apt
Sunday: L'Isle-sur-la-Sorgue

As soon as we had settled in at the beginning of this month we had reviewed the Tuesday market up in Gordes to scan the stalls snuggled against the Vasarely castle, and to get a feeling for this summer's merchandise. Nuts and olives. Sausages and cheeses. Old books and periodicals. Weaving and jewelry and pottery. But now that August fast approaches, the Gordes market has become flooded with tourists and is impenetrable. Despite the flashy parking lot installed as a catchall for vehicular overflow and where we first saw the folk dancers last Sunday, the town appears virtually under siege. We steer clear of Gordes on Tuesdays now.

Although Sunday is market day in L'Isle, I persuaded Moth to ignore the anticipated crowds because today the market also coincides with an annual *brocantes* of some renown, and I have a couple of wedding presents on my to-do list. Despite traffic, Moth inveigled a parking spot behind the Système U with her usual aplomb and we headed on foot towards the cathedral through a circuitous shortcut hoping to emerge in the center of the flea-market area. But surprise! We discovered instead the entire town center closed to cars and decorated for a Marché Provençal à l'Ancien. The streets were banked with tall bundles of freshly scythed bamboo, and huge sunny seed-swollen sunflowers were tied together into giant columns beside every shop. Potted cypress trees and sheaves of hay and aromatic stashes of lavender in full bloom were gathered under long red-and-yellow silky banners clipped into swallowtails like gift ribbons, strung across overhead from house to house between balconies whose usual attire of drying T-shirts and denim overalls had been removed for the occasion.

Individual shops set up tableaux in the street in front of their doorways to show how their trades might have been practiced long ago. Outside the laundromat an enormous galvanized tub filled to the brim with water and linens left to soak stood next to an arrangement of clay amphora, or water jugs, a washboard, and a pounding stone. A fabric shop offered demonstrations in carding wool and spinning thread on the wheel, and a *parfumerie* displayed essences in fragile, bubbled-blue glass vials which had been handblown over a hundred years ago. Each merchant was assisted by his or her whole family, all dressed, like the folk dancers we saw last Sunday, in provençal costume. The littlest girls, no more than four or five years old, handed us sprigs of lavender to sniff at as we strolled.

The market in L'Isle spreads out in a loopy figure eight along four streets which converge, at the waist of the eight, at the cathedral square. A new and novel accent along the route, and one which appears to be a staple in many villages this year, is a small loudspeaker

in the shape of a tin can; these are affixed to every intersection within earshot of the commercial district. Last evening as we drove through Gordes, raucous rock tunes ricocheted off the walls of the Vasarely castle interrupted at intervals by bulletins announcing the merits of local restaurants and shops. This morning the music here suited a

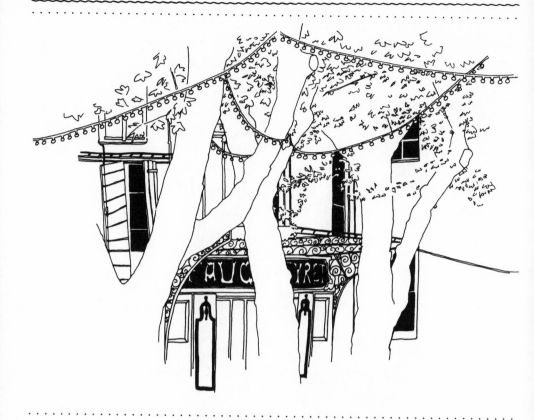

promenade, just low-key jazz and easy-listening—and at a far lower
decibel level. But because local ordinances prohibit possession of
farm animals because their braying, mooing, and bleating disturb
the public, how long will the same public tolerate these more per-
sistently clamorous loudspeakers?

As we made our way through the market, we looked closely at
the mélange of goods so prettily disposed in this provençal display.
The umbrellas sheltering the foodstalls were threaded with sunflowers and bamboo and lavender, and more lavender was thrust into
doorways along the route. As the lavender harvest falls at the end
of the month, just a week away, the blossoms no longer appear a

deep, dark purple but have begun to bleach out, to pale in anticipation of being cut. Our pungent little sprigs remind us that the field beyond our house is ripe for harvest, too.

Under the fluttering fat-fringed and colorful umbrellas, all pink and blue and green and yellow in candy-cane combinations, bread and fruit and nuts and herbs and grains and sausages sing silent succulent siren songs to all who pass by. First: the olives. Olives in plastic-lined twiggy baskets, swimming in brine with thick hand-hewn ladles at the ready. Olives: black and brown and green, fat and narrow, smooth-fleshed and wrinkled. Olives: studded with pimientos, accompanied by wedges and slices of tart lemon. Olives mashed into *tapenade,* a thick luscious spread mixed with anchovy and pine nuts and oil and garlic and onion—ready to trowel onto a slab of crusty baguette or simply lick off the fingers.

And nuts: peanuts, salted or demurely plain; and cashews, curvaceous horseshoe morsels, beckoning from their bin; pistachios smiling pink between pursed piny lips.

Grains: couscous, small and medium and grand; and bulgur, staples for the migrant workers from Algeria who pull in the harvest in these parts and then hang out on Sundays outside the Système U.

Seeds: sunflower and sesame.

Herbs: dried or lush and live in clay pots ready for garden or window sill. Herbs: medicinal *verveine* to cosset the stomach or liver or kidneys or throat. *Tussilage* as antidote to asthma. *Camomille* to calm and soothe the nerves. And the potted herbs, which sound so melodic in French: *basilic* and *persil* and *ciboulette* and *oseille* and *romarin* and, of course, *lavande*.

And breads: today, shawled in provençal cottons or handkerchiefs or toweling, and annotated on doilies with their calligraphically penned names. Yeast breads and olive breads and anchovy breads and nut breads and basil breads and breads redolent of *herbes de Provence*. Plus braided breads and chubby humpbacked breads and long cross-slashed breads and elegant narrow baguettes and fat wreath-shaped breads.

And how about ice-cream cones—*cornets*—alluringly empty, awaiting *glace* or sorbet? Plain handkerchief-rolled cones or waffle-weave double-scoops or prick-edged raspberry-tinted sorbet cones or, best of all, supersized gridded sugar cones already dipped in dark chocolate, gaping, expectant, yearning for a fantasia scoop.

Cavaillon melons, small enough to cradle in the palm, and bursting at their navels and fragrant with a cantaloupy scent. Garlic braids. *Cornichons*. Peaches and tomatoes and lettuces and eggplants. Hams, and pâtés of duck, and terrines.

Not only foods, though, but gadgets, such as the Mickey Mouse–eared can opener I buy each visit for cat food cans back in the States, and tools and toys and clothes. We pass piles of espadrilles, twine-tied by size and color. Plastic jellies and crazy hightop sneakers fancifully painted in bizarre, punk-inspired designs. Shuffle shoes and thongs and *pantoufle* bedroom slippers like Moth's. Totes with FELIX

THE CAT and HOLLYWOOD and the ubiquitous BENETTON. Hats emblazoned with automobile logos and, of course, T-shirts.

As we passed through the glorious array, between the sunflowers and bamboos and olives and melons, Moth stopped by a small table where a craftsman flame-branded round wooden napkin rings and she bought four, for Bill and Bo and David and Pierre. And I unhooked two pairs of outrageously colored bermuda-length shorts for the boys off the spokes of an umbrella. All the rage this year, these shorts flash strident neon hues, each leg in a different screaming pattern. David's shone Day-Glo yellow-and-black stripes along one leg and violet palm trees on the other, while Peter's blazed pink and green and black and yellow checkers on one side and pink X-ray charts across the center seam. Moth asks the inevitable question: Will my sons, conservative in taste, wear them?

Emerging from the cornucopian cocoon of booths and stalls to the river's edge, we were startled to find ourselves in the thick of a pageant: the Fête de Pêche à l'Ancien—a fishing spectacle. Half a dozen longboats, like punts, floated into view. Needle-nose fore and hatchback aft, these dark wooden barques were poled by fishermen done up in adaptive garb: white shirts rolled to the elbow and pants rolled to the knee, vests from Sunday suits and wide red cummerbunds and kerchiefs tied, pirate-style, behind the ear. Some carried tridents and others hoopskirted nets which looked like mesh lampshades, and still others slung long cages fabricated of twigs.

L'Isle-sur-la-Sorgue—straddling ancillary canals and the river for which it is named—has been called the Venice of Provence and takes her aquarian heritage seriously. Her streets are named for creatures of the deep: Rue de l'Anguille, the eel; de la Truite, the trout; de l'Ecrevisse, the crayfish. And water long powered her traditional industries of clothmaking, tanning, and dyeing. In the thirteenth century, forty-six waterwheels roiled her waters; only a few mossy survivors remain.

So here are the fishermen, plunging tridents at slippery mercurial river trout, flashing their catch into the twig cages and lampshade nets, while onlookers, three-deep along either side of the water, shriek halleluiahs.

After watching awhile, we bridged the canal and walked on to the flea market. Here, engravings and camisoles and fringed towels and assorted ceramics and glass and silver and gemstones were interspersed amongst a miscellany of seen-better-days furnishings. Dealers know too well the lure of the flea market, and it seems everything of real value has been snapped up. But the linens are a good buy and I found two pretty pillow shams for the promised wedding presents on the way back to the Souris.

Midday: After the flash and tumble of the fair and "Pêche," we almost forgot a reservation Moth had made for lunch at a little inn up in Venasque, a tiny hill-village located a few kilometers beyond the Abbaye de Senanque in the gorges near Mont Ventoux. We hustled the Souris out of the crowds and back towards Gordes. Venasque lies about halfway through a mountain pass, on a detour off the road, and is best known for its tranquil seventh-century baptistery which is one of the most ancient religious buildings in France and which we make a point to see on each visit. Each time, we have been greeted by an elderly caretaker, wizened almost to Peter's height, who, summoned by a little bell, carefully, respectfully opened the door with a long wrought-iron key. Each time we came, he parceled out peppermints to the boys and left us with a small typewritten sheet to be read in the silence on our own. Today, a huge garish sign announces Open Hours in six languages and the caretaker is nowhere in evidence. Fame may overwhelm this little sanctuary at last.

Ascending the steep road to the village fountain and square where we'd find the inn where we were to lunch, we noticed all the little enticements which are sure to lure *étrangers*. We know already that the reputation of the chef reaches far beyond the confines of this tiny village and that he now offers suites to rent over his restaurant, complete with television and room service. A little potteryworks we've patronized in the past has revived its charming cherry-decorated façade with new paint; it won't be long before the pottery will appear in American outlets. A visit into the shop, Le Temps des Cerises, which is a combination atelier and salesroom, reconfirmed the quality of the handmodeled clayworks. Dishes and pitchers and tiny vessels to hold essence of lavender sit in the windows, and similar pieces can be made by custom order. Bold blue checks or dots surrounding freehand outlines of animals are a favorite design motif, as are pale-petaled blossoms and dots in mauve, both on a pure white ground. Unlike the *poteries* in Dieulefit which respond to modish designs, Le Temps des Cerises retains its original pottery shapes and idiosyncratic motifs, but we could not help but note that prices have escalated, in keeping with those all over France. This summer offers few bargains against the slipping dollar.

The Auberge de la Fontaine takes its name, logically and prettily enough, from the triple-tier, cake-shaped fountain which dominates the village square. Its dining room, on the "first" floor, or second level, faces the square through petunia-girdled windows; our chef graciously offered us a table close to the glass where the sun poured through the petals as through stained-glass onto our laps.

Sunday luncheon is a ritual the French enjoy to the utmost, and many families make it a weekly habit to eat out, both as a treat and as a way to gather generations together. The Auberge, compactly laid out in two rooms, bustled with families drawing their tables close together to encourage companionable conversation. We were glad to have made our reservation far in advance. The chef and his

wife circulated amongst the tables, greeting their guests and explaining the simple menu. One eats what they decide to cook that day—
in the style called *table d'hôte*—and so their written menu charmingly,
if enigmatically, takes a neutral position: all courses, except the entrée
choice announced by the chef, are called *mystères*! The mystery to
start turned out to be a *tapenade* followed by cool marbles of assorted
melon and a *confit* of warm duck presented on mixed greens dashed
with vinaigrette. We both selected the entrée of rabbit dressed with
cassis, or black currants.

Moth's chosen beverage on this and other outings always chal-
lenges the chef; because she can no longer drink wine, she asks for
iced coffee—an aberration each and every chef volubly disdains. But

Moth holds firm and, gauntlet thrown, each chef eventually formulates a concoction. Once it was a *frivolité glacée,* an iced sweet treat; on another occasion the coffee came in the guise of a Margarita, in a stemmed glass rimmed with sugar. Today, though, the chef brought a glass of coffee and a glass of ice and Moth was beseeched to mix her own.

25 July

O
n these *tout fermé* Mondays Moth and I hole in to write letters.
Moth sets aside time every day to write, but I hoard my time and
feel freer for postcards and letters when there are no outside obligations or errands to consider. When I returned to the States to
complete high school and to attend college, I enjoyed the weekly
ritual of sending news and anecdotes of friends to Moth and Dad
remaining behind in Florence. My journeys home were few then,
just for the summer, and letter-writing was our link, our connection.
It feels good to revive this ritual to connect to Bill and David and
Peter and to the office and to friends.

Peter has been sending over little notes and sketches from camp,
outlining cabin and camp on a map so that we can visualize his
whereabouts as he moves from one activity to another. Both he and
David are architecturally oriented, and build great cities of Lego and
blocks. They contrive elaborate floor plans on graph paper and create
futuristic cities where the air and water will be pure, the trees lean
and strong, and the industries nonpolluting. They'd never give up
automobiles though!

David and Bill do not write and never have; they prefer words of the mouth to words on the page. We've been reading of the seemingly ceaseless heat wave in New York—over thirty days in the 90s so far—and I imagine them both lying inert with FatCat Tom stretching his twenty feline pounds between them.

26 July

In the still deep of the night, when the waxing moon sprinkled mercury sparkles onto our terrace, I was awakened by the persistent sound of splashing, like a waterfall. Could it be Philippe, given to mood swings, swimming back and forth, lap after insomniac lap? I did not want to investigate this possibility, for his eyes sidle and dart, and would his humor match the moon-bitten night?

We have, we thought, arrived at a convenient and unspoken schedule for our swimming—and Philippe's. Philippe and his sister, who tends to his cyclical sadnesses, like to sunbathe fully naked and they take their nude dips midmorning while we are at work or off on errands. Philippe makes a second dash into the pool as the sun recedes behind Jean and Chouchou's silhouetted hamlet. I crawl windmill laps at midday to shrug off collage concentration, followed by Moth's plunge and Dad's own crawl just before lunch. Acquaintances drop by to cool off in the late afternoon, and so comings and goings in the nine-stroke pool, like interlacings, weave through the day. But tonight? Well, I did not explore and instead slumped back into shallow-rippled dreams until dawn.

Exploring the situation at sunrise, I felt completely foolish, for the water geysered only because the tail of Michael's chunky little cir-

culating pool filter had pretzeled on itself creating a sputtering spout over the stone archway between the pool and our terrace and lawn. The pool level is down five inches, but a lean swath of lawn glistens— and all for my lack of courage!

Today Dad returned from California and so we went off to fetch him at the TGV. As we awaited his arrival, we took a Perrier in a small café just outside the train station and watched the comings and goings in the adjoining parking lot. An enormous caravan, or RV, attempted to pass through the departure tollgate. Rocking and heaving its elephantine bulk through the narrow passage, the caravan shimmied and jerked in spurts of intensifying frustration and hysteria. Everyone in our café lounged back, as if at a movie showing, muttering subtitles and "*mon dieus*" at the obese machine. Assorted Renaults and Citroëns, cousins to our Souris, piled up behind. Toots and obscenities punctuated the heat—the tollbooth operator shrugged impassively. When, at last, the caravan popped through, everyone cheered—until, *holà,* five minutes later, *ha!* another caravan identical to the first and, again, the same driver. Rerun.

Dad, glazed with his two-plane, one-train, twenty-hour return, asked that we rush him home so that he could sleep. In fact, I have felt no particular desire to return to Avignon to tour anyway this year. Like Goldilocks, I've tried out towns throughout the region until I've found ones that feel Just Right. Avignon is just too big! I prefer the medium-sized towns—Apt, Cavaillon, Carpentras, and L'Isle-sur-la-Sorgue. Ringed by plane-tree-shaded boulevards—where there were once fortifications—these towns focus inward, within the pleasant rotary, to a clutch of narrow byways connected to a few promenade shopping streets which then converge upon a genial market square with a few umbrella-fringed cafés. Also: unimposing churches with paintings by minor artists "of the Avignon School." An art gallery or two, a good bookstore, bakeries and butchers. A few simple dress shops and an electronics store. A florist. A place to purchase *boules*. And nothing ever too chic or too *cher*.

Of course we have played tourist in these towns, and in Avignon too, because we wanted to see everything and do everything and enjoy everything . . . but that was our first visit. We probed the Palais des Papes, where the Popes held court for over half a century, from 1309 until 1377, before returning the papacy to Rome. And we rode a tinkling toy train up to the gardens overlooking the sawed-off bridge canonized in the *chanson:*

> *Sur le pont d'Avignon*
> *On y danse, on y danse,*
> *Sur le pont d'Avignon*
> *On y danse, tout en rond.*

But this year I am intent on avoiding the tourist spots and tourists—and, I confess, my own kind. This is a Goldilocks summer, for feeling Just Right.

And this journal, too, to feel Just Right, is becoming something different; it is neither so sketchy nor so conversational as the two I wrote before. This summer I want to dive into my foreignness here and into my Americanness, to think about languages both familiar and elusive, and recline amongst easy and uncluttered words, to find who I may be as a writer on holiday and a writer just listening and a writer just writing for whatever reason the day brings, and outside the convention of work-words. Like Joan with her dolphins, I want to swim into the buzz of words and find out what I can remember of a forgotten phrase or a misplaced idiom or a lapsed argot. This summer is an archeological time for chipping and chipping and chipping. What words have a hold on me? Where does my own poetry reside?

I am most comfortable with asides and glances, fragments of phrases, snippets, like the collage panes I am stitching into quilts. I am most comfortable, I know, behind whatever window I make. I like looking out at my world. I am comfortable within the window, too, within context and not totally alone. I am durably stitched into the fabric of family and a few and furiously intimate friends. I could not sit on a desert floor and stare at an unceasing sky without them.

I don't know the people here too well. I don't know that I really want to. I like the comfort of easy acquaintance bordering on anonymity that a summer like this brings. Ricocheting amongst these people and loving them a little inside the boundaries of this place and this summer feels Just Right for now. I will return to good friends soon.

And so I swim my laps, nine strokes to and nine back, and listen to the edges of the pool press tidal murmurs under my bathing cap; the water rose its five inches while we were in Avignon and it's my turn before lunch.

27 July

Rest and recuperation for Dad, rest and reading for Moth, and rest and retooling for me! And, late in the afternoon, a quiet lemonade in the café in Goult.

28 July

Because the Souris was to spend the day down in Les Beaumettes for her tune-up, Peggy offered to transport Moth and me in her sleek white Citroën—the kind that resembles a vacuum cleaner, or a stingray—to St.-Rémy so that Moth could visit her favorite Souleïado and I a pretty linens shop. Once exiting our valley and crossing the Durance River, the road to St.-Rémy plunges, direct and without interruption, under a vast nave of plane trees, glorious this summer in full leafy Afros and narrow white stockings pulled taut against their blotched bark trunks to repel pests and to alert drivers at night to the danger of swerving off the road. We circled the boulevard around to the market square and parked there easily within sight of a café where Peggy could retreat from the sun under an umbrella with a coffee while we completed our errands.

This town, well known for its *herbes de Provence,* is better known still for the asylum where van Gogh, trapped in the roller-coaster urgencies of his mind, pursued his relentless explosions of pen and paint. His daubs thickened here, and his colors tore into violent intensities, and the mistral momentum of tree and grassblade and cloud and star surged out of control, out of his eyes and into a catastrophic infinity.

Windows, edges and limits, frames and constraints, conflicts:

piercing convention in order to be able to be solitary for a time, and joyfully alone, yet retaining a context that must include job and family—this, for me, is a struggle at home. I may never dare the outside of the window, for I fear the oceanic void beyond the boundaries. I close my eyes and feel myself plunge into perpetual abyss, flame into perpetual migraine, into unremitting blindness. When I was a child, a doctor operated on my eyes, to reroute muscle, and when I awoke, it was to darkness, remote and wet. Sometimes I feel that blackness will engulf me still, if I try to look too deep or intensely into anything. And in that blackness I sense a madness as haunting and overpowering as van Gogh's.

So I wear my family, perhaps, like sunshades, to protect me from too much light and too much dark. Family is asylum, and asylum a seductively protective frame.

Moving into another language or into verse or into mathematical ellipse or musical sonority or danceleap or daubed canvas urges the artist into the bright light of trance, a magnificent, translucent, joyous trance, but then as the momentum builds, the artist presses closer and closer to edges both real and fantastical. And, ultimately, to a beyond, what beyond, madness?

I remember taking a class with an art teacher in Florence who made me swing my arms in wide arcs before lifting pencil or brush, admonishing me to abandon myself to the vital vortex she outlined in her own arcs, swirling from head to heart in three spiral side-winding volutions, to return with a grand, grinning straight rush back up to the head again. She believed this continuous path of energy unleashed all creative impulse, a magnanimous gesture coiling passion and insight into one huge stretch. Breathe deeply, she counseled, and then reach, reach as far as you can and then, and only then: paint.

How to harness, exalt, enjoy, and transform these arcs into adventure and not into hallucinatory haze requires an enormous reserve of energy and control. It is the control that transposes that centrifugal riptide of passion into a salutary vortex of creativity. But what if that energy surges out of control? And when? It's the edges that confuse me: Just how elastic are they? How responsive? How tolerant? When creative energy pushes harder, and harder still, against the edges of the vortex, can it only explode?

I observe my father pull back from the edge, like me, to tidy chord and meticulous melody, picking his way across a clean page with a perfectly pointed pencil. And I watch my mother stay cautious inside the confines of her inkline and camera angle. What would happen to Dad if, like a dog, he heard tones our inadequate ears resist or, like a bird, trillings beyond our conscious grasp or, like Joan's dolphins, sonics our skins can only swim alongside? What if he allowed his music to pulse into a wild beyond? Did Mozart accelerate to the other side of sound? Did van Gogh course into colors we cannot code?

I left my Florentine art teacher before I learned to breathe deeply enough, returning to the States to the courteous code of a boarding school. Away from the consolation of her confidence I retreated into the discreet discipline of rote. So when I get caught up in an idea now, it darts out of my slippery grip as fast as a Sorgue fish. I cannot tag it fast enough it seems. I squeeze at it, like a droplet, out through the thick and spongy tissue of my brain as through a pastry tube, and only hope it will dapple and scroll, and finally sliptrail into word or collage as paint onto a slab of raw faïence. I distill in measured dimples of thought; I am not intimate with vagrant possibilities. I hold my breath.

29 July

W̲e awoke to gloom. Or so it seemed. From the bedroom windows the sky appeared perfectly blue and free of cloud over the recumbent Lubéron. Yet upon opening the Juliet doors to the bathroom balcony, I noticed a huge glowering thundercloud hunkered grossly aslant our rooftop and across the hayloft. Directly above, the sky divided as if scissored, blue to gray, like a theatrical and sad/happy mask, one half in smile and one in tears. Which will it be today?

The weather so far has been close to perfect. After the mistral over the Quatorze Juillet, each day has opened lucid, vivid after blanket-nights and has closed in drunken sunset. Nor have we felt any sweat-sodden noons. The hottest part of each day, from two until five or so, slams dry and prickly into the house and we draw the French doors to the bright white terrace and pull the curtains to shade the living room. Then we read or nap in dimness until the heat fractures. And so far it always does.

The sun won today, sending the gray on over to Apt, and so Moth proposed a photography tour to look at farmhouse shapes after breakfast, before the colors diffused into their customary heat-haze. As we drive here and there throughout the valley, special images have connected, but fleetingly, and we've been waiting for a morning to record some of our favorites. I have begun sketching as an alternative to the collages, and I want to supplement drawings with photos as material for the journal.

Moth makes a point, too, of pausing each summer to collect the images she has assembled behind her eyes, then seeks them out and transfers them to film to fill her memory books back home; I make scrapbooks too. She has an uncanny knack for recall, remembering the exact location of the subjects she desires, and she drives with unerring accuracy from one site to the next. She's a cardsharp too, and unbeatable at games, and this same precise capacity for remembering what is important and eliminating the rest has always informed and illuminated her photography.

Neither of us belongs to the dawn-and-dusk "atmosphere" school which imprints rosy landscapes with silhouettes as a matter of course; we can purchase exquisite art cards for these images. We are content to amble forth after breakfast.

Directing photo shoots back home has made me lazy; I take a cavalier attitude towards film and I have grown accustomed to waste. Photographers today, using motorized equipment, peel off dozens of images, shifting aperture and speed slightly from one frame to the next to ensure one or two useful exposures. Film is cheap, they say. And they aid their efforts with dozens of Polaroids to check on lighting. Moth, by contrast, learned to trust her eye, never a light meter. She scans the sky and composes her shot, then snap. That's that. She does not tolerate waste. Every shot, she was taught, must count. When I was young she took me photographing and I would watch her, and try to emulate her technique. She carried an enormously heavy Mamiyaflex and I had my Brownie Hawkeye and then a small 35mm carry-about. It is a treat to accompany her again as she tests her eye.

On the Coustellet road we stopped before a long low farmhouse stuccoed to paled taupe and rasped by mistral for so long its hide crackled. A scatter of tiny faded green louvred shutters nicked into the façade. Further along, zigzagging back towards Gordes, we shot a cheerful homestead, painted bubblegum with kelly shutters and an azure door and an ancient orange Citroën Deux Chevaux, like a tin gumdrop, parked out front. And two plastic *piscines*, upended like dolmens, flashed their brazen aqua cavities to the road in hopes they would captivate us to purchase. At this hour many fields are under irrigation before the heat, and water arabesqued feathery gossamer veils of spray in liquid slow-motion over the thirsty vegetables.

Back home: Drama! Our first scorpion of the summer. While scrubbing the bathroom floor, I upended one behind the toilet. Tiny and black and impenitent, it flaunted and clicked its miniature lobster-claws and skittered behind a sponge. I halted its detour to the tub with a long dose of insecticide. But now I'm brought up short: Must I give up the bliss of bare feet? Scorpions invade damp corners every summer. We have expected them and perhaps the scissored sky was

a signal to their arrival. This one heralds the coming of others. The pale, colorless ones can kill. This black once could incur serious illness, but the sting would not prove fatal—or so we are told. In any case, we dread them.

Otherwise, the "wildlife" of the house has been rather tame and amusing. Our downstairs loo has been occupied for days by an obese mottled spider and an equally immense near-translucent cricket, facing off one against the other in the stall shower. Neither has moved. The spider has drawn up its long legs under its bloated belly, and the cricket, not to be outdone, copycats its position. We have dubbed them Tyson and Spinks after the boxers back in the States. Moth, a firm believer in letting nature take its course, counsels against smashing them and I fear I am not brave enough to tackle them anyway. Dad mutters about removing them to the outdoors via a glass and cardboard, but has made no move to do so. And Moth wonders aloud what Michael's next houseparty, a group of chic American friends from Long Island due to arrive the week after Moth and Dad leave, would say if they found the beasts still in residence!

The wasps have multiplied with ferocity in the roof tiles that serve as their summer hotel, and they make their way through the long screens protecting the French doors to the bedroom balcony that spans the Lubéron side of the house. This afternoon I tried to darn in a mesh over a scraggly hole with needle and thread to thwart the largest bombers. The sewing kit read NICOLETT ISLAND INN—MINNEAPOLIS; how distant that seems today!

Unfortunately, too, the arrival of insect hordes also revives my fear of terrorism and the unknown and I begin to feel anxious again about my return flight. Like some chronic wound, anxiety surfaces; the scorpion is a reminder of evils which our "simple life" compassionately and conveniently circumvents. I feel shaken, as I do when I glance over the crazy juxtapositions of advertisement to editorial in a newspaper: Diamond "tennis bracelets" alongside miners suffocating to death in South Africa; mink coats rubbing against body counts of endangered species or statistics of human starvation; multimillion-dollar real estate listings packed in behind photographs

of squatters' dwellings and per capita incomes of under 100 dollars—
if that; grocery coupons aligned with record droughts and famine
reports. Newspapers are monuments to irony.

Evening: This afternoon, Béatrice, a friend from Canada who summers with her Swiss mother in a neighboring hamlet, dropped in
with her two young sons for a swim. We hadn't seen each other in
four years and decided on the spot to catch up on news and families
over dinner in Cabrières. A local hangout, the Bistrot de Michel,
caters to a bar crowd on the street level, but up behind the kitchen
a simple graveled terrace gathers diners around a dozen tables under
a few umbrellas. The day's menu offered simple fare, just an antipasto
salad, a hunk of lamb, a *tarte*.

Eating out with a contemporary, like this, is something I've not
done this summer and it feels good to talk about our different lives
in different cities, our similar concerns about juggling children and
work, husbands who can take little time off, parents in our lives.
But also Béatrice's work interests me—bilingual, she acts as a simultaneous translator for the Canadian government, traveling to
meetings whenever summoned. I wonder at her fluency, but also at
her ease in translating nuance and mood, intention and inflection,
not just the words themselves—and at such speed. "Lost in translation" is the severest problem in the world today. How to ascertain,
and perceive, and comprehend, not simply the mere meaning of
words, but the brush of the hand across the brow, the slight glimmer
in the eye, the nod or bow? The implication of juxtaposition speaks
more than the words, just as the ads in tandem with text do in our
newspapers. Translation, it seems, is a judgment of senses, the visual
and the tactile as well as what can be heard. And it is all too human,
so vulnerable to error.

Béatrice's face glows with her sensibility to shades and tones.
Radiant and alert, she speaks with her children with the gentle firm-
ness I can imagine in her translations. As we ponder our effect on
our children as mothers who work, and how we influence them with
summers here or with trips, we ask: Will we fuel their curiosity for

people who live differently than we do; will they honor feelings that are dissimilar to ours; will they tolerate other beliefs, other cultures, other faiths? Will they grow up with a sensibility to environment, for art, for the deep shades of history? Will they be able to translate, life to life, across the boundaries of nations?

Time overlaps time and I talk of David, tugging at his independence at fifteen and then reeling in to family as he straddles his worlds, childhood and manhood; is he ready to leave us and go out on his own? I remember Florence again, running to our home and away, running out to sing and running out to dance and to see the opera and to suck on long strands of tomato-coated spaghetti, to return only to sleep between the tendril tiles outside our garret room, and longing, always longing, too. How have I translated my childhood to womanhood, or translated my own longing to my son's, or my own life to his? That luxury of being in between, safe in the embrace of family and independent enough to move about, that is truly a treasure, but when we were teenagers, my sisters and I, we did not appreciate the indulgence—typical teenagers we! I am glad to have the chance to relive some "teenaged" freedom once again this summer with my parents, and feel the real between of straddling two ages, fourteen and forty-four, in simultaneous translation.

30 *July*

The click-click-click of the tractor harvesting our lavender field relieves us of wondering if and when the lavender would be cut this year. We had heard that the farmer, like our village patriarch, had taken ill and the field this summer looked rather dispirited and unkempt, interspersed as it was with Queen Anne's lace and weeds poking up through the lavender rows. So the tractor reassures us. We hoped for this harvest all week. The pacific percussions and sniffs of lavender scent float into the house like zephyrs and we decide—in some extrasensory way, without discussion—to remain home and listen, and relax over our projects and reading.

From the balcony off our bedrooms we can see the tractor rolling through the field. The thick clumps or bales of lavender stalks will be deposited astride the pruned rows which look, from this distance, hedgehoggy in their new brush cut.

Each year we gather in our own bundles of lavender and strip them of their bud-like blossoms to fill big deep glazed milkbowls we then place on tables throughout the house to ward off mosquitoes and other insects. I also pull the fragrant buds to make sachets for friends back home. Two years ago my boss gave me long snips of Liberty of London cotton lawn, a thin cloth, and I cut these into patchwork squares and sewed them up into chunky little pillows. The fragrance lasts and lasts.

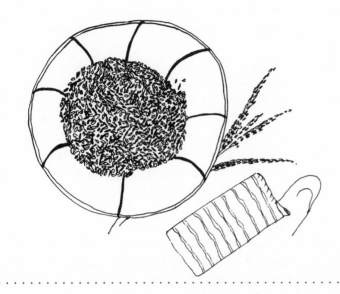

Of all herbs, lavender may be the most beloved, the most popular, and the most romantic. Thriving in the intense sun of the Mediterranean, lavender was revered early on by Egyptians and Arabs and by Greeks and Romans, who gave it a name based upon washing—*lavare,* to wash—because they, and I too, enjoyed scenting their bathwater with this pungently aromatic herb. During the Middle Ages, lavender was considered something of an aphrodisiac—although, conversely, it was also said to be used to ensure chastity.

Lavender was accepted as an antiseptic to disinfect bites and wounds, as an astringent for the skin, and as an ingredient in smelling salts to revive those prone to fainting fits. Rodale's *Illustrated Encyclopedia of Herbs* adds a few additional and bizarre uses, including its application in embalming corpses and as a scent to tame lions. Lavender has rarely been thought of as a culinary herb, although recipes for venison occasionally recommend adding a sprig of lavender to the sauce.

Lavender these days is typically distilled into oil for use in perfumes, soaps, bath oils and salts. One acre of lavender will yield about fifteen pounds of oil. We gratefully receive our house's allotment of oil, which we preserve in graceful antique glass vials in our bathrooms.

In the past we have driven into the mountains beyond Apt to see one of the last remaining handcranked local distilleries at work. The rudely constructed machine operates almost in the same primitive manner as an antique cider press and appears almost as crude. Most lavender these days is processed, by contrast, in giant factories because the demand for the herb is so great. In fact, a lavender sachet is the single most favored souvenir of the region, bagged in chipper provençal cloth and tied up with ribbon.

Also today we pluck at the garden which now teems with tomatoes, zucchini, and eggplant. At last Moth can make her ratatouille! Our onion sets, bearded red oblongs, rest on the kitchen sill under the knotted end of the clothesline and press their rosy skins against the weathered aqua of the shutters.

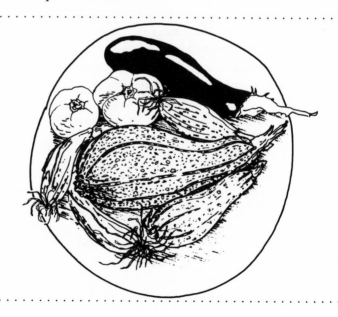

MOTH'S RAT

Chop one or two unpeeled zucchini any which way into a large bowl. Sauté the chopped zucchini, by handfuls, in sputtering olive oil with *herbes de Provence* to taste in a large long-handled and heavy saucepan. Ditto an unpeeled eggplant, chopping it coarsely first into the large bowl after the zucchini have been removed to the pan. Add the eggplant to the zucchini. Ditto a large peeled red onion, diced. Add fresh basil leaves for color. Peel and chop three or four fresh tomatoes and add to the mixture. Cook all until soft but not mushy, about ten to fifteen minutes. Let sit, or refrigerate, and reheat for dinner.

Moth cooks by feel and look and taste, sensing her proportions by dabbling about with a spoon and tasting as she goes. With a painterly instinct, she balances one vegetable against the other. If ten minutes is too short a cooking interval, she lets her rat cook a bit longer. If there are more than three of us for dinner, she adds more vegetables. *Ça va.* And it is delicious!

31 *July, Sunday*

This, our fourth Sunday, marks the beginning of my last full week here. August is upon us. I depart two Tuesdays hence. Dad has begun to set aside time away from his Casio keyboard and his composition to practice his Cole Porter program on Michael's grand piano over in the hayloft for the August 5 fête and now, suddenly, the date presses insistently upon us.

Moth and I left him early to his ivory tickling, to drive over to the nearby village of Lagnes. Today Lagnes celebrates its annual Grande Foire Provençale, another provençal fair, and Moth thought it an opportune time to pay a visit to the *santonnier. Santons,* provençal Nativity figures, can be found in any local gift shop, but the Lagnes *santonnier* receives callers in his atelier. Each year Moth adds to her collection of *santons,* and this year, expects to complete her set.

Even at 9 A.M. the Place de Mairie, the town hall square, and contiguous streets were packed and booths primed. In front of the *mairie* itself, dancers in jester hats and Big Bird–like costumes homemade of overlapping polychrome flaps were parading around, swinging their arms and grabbing at the pretty girls in the crowd. A merry-go-round circled gaily, spinning a miniature car, bus, house, and boat, and we watched as a cherubic boy of around seven grabbed a bright tassel. A horse fair set up at the periphery of the fair, just beyond a double booth selling flame-branded saddles and bridles, offered rides on small ponies to the rest of the children. Lined up alongside, other, larger steeds looked to be tagged for sale.

We moved directly through the displays of herbs and soaps and jellyshoes and T-shirts and dried flowers to the *santonnier*'s studio, easy to identify because he always sets out a large rag doll wearing cast-off rubber gloves on a stool out front to announce *Ici*—here!

The *santonnier* works in a rude shed behind his equally simple homestead, with a turning wheel, molds, paints, and kiln always stoked. A complete Nativity, set up behind glass, displays the forty-nine figures in his repertory and the half-dozen or so dwellings he has devised to house the Holy Family and attendant villagers. Each figure represents a typical Provençal, each with a sharply defined character and story to tell. The *santonnier* states with pride that he knows each character as intimately as if he or she were a friend or relative.

The crèche, as he describes it, originated in 1223 with St. Francis of Assisi, patron saint and protector of living creatures; but *santons* were not made here in Provence until after the French Revolution. Prior to the Revolution, Provençaux enacted the Living Crèche each Christmas, celebrating the birth of Christ in a tableau. At the time of the Revolution, the French government tried to suppress this expression of Christmas faith as heresy, but the rebellious craftspeople began to mold their beloved Holy Family and their friends in miniature, out of wood—and often even out of bread—to set up in their homes during the Holy Season. When the terror ceased, Living Crèches were revived; the manufacture of *santons* continued too, though now the figures are rendered in clay.

Imagine, he writes in his brochure,

> these *santons* as alive, living happily in this little village where everyone knows them, where their friendships as well as their animosities mark their relationships. Here comes my great-grandfather, a fisherman of the Sorgue, and his wife who sold fishes in the church square at L'Isle-sur-la-Sorgue; and my grandfather, both hunter

and poacher, who traipsed over the *garrigues* until his death; and my friend, the gypsy, who stops by each year on his way south to the Gypsy Festival in Saintes-Maries-de-la-Mer on the sea. If I didn't know these characters so well I would never have taken on this line of work.

Christmas is a fête of renewal, when every child who is born is our dearest hope; and Christmas is also a fête of generosity, a generosity our poor world sorely needs. Our little clay figures are happy, quite simply, with the life they have been given. They have no need for great words or grand gestures; they remain humble. Or, rather, they retain a simplicity that comes from being free. In this world, evil is converted to good, and the avaricious open their purses, and enemies become reconciled. . . .

When I awake and see the sun rising behind these hills, behind my corral, I tell myself how lucky I am to live in this world that I love so and which, for one short moment, I can share with you.

The *santonnier* recognized Moth at once and fell into excited conversation with her about the figures she wanted to see, about her crèche and how she sets it up back in the States, about her summer, about this very beautiful day for a fair, yes?

SOME *SANTONS*

Mary and Joseph and Baby Jesus in his bed of hay
The ox and the ass
The shepherds and their sheep
The Three Wise Men and their camels
The miller with a sack of flour upon his shoulder

The fisherman with his rod and the hunter with his gun
The old lady carrying a bundle of twigs for the fire
The blind man being led by his godson
The elderly couple who have been married for a very long time
The washerwoman pounding a sheet upon a stone

The waterbearer and the man who carries a jug of wine
The drummer and the dancers and the fiddler and the bassist

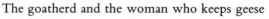

The goatherd and the woman who keeps geese
The knifesharpener
The knitter
The gardener
The baker
The glazier
The optimist and the simpleton

Who would we be in the tableau? We are neither so simple nor so defined, with our city ways and cluttered consciousness. I know that I could not give up everything to knit or keep geese, nor even to just make collages or write at whim. Despite my protestations of the summer and deep love and deeper yearning for this Simple Life, I know I can be easily seduced by some fine material thing, a lovely linen pillow-slip perhaps, or how about a computer!

In college a friend brought a gift I cherish and keep on my wall so that I can see it every day, a quotation torn from a book and set in a gilt frame, found at a flea market, and which guides me always:

MY SYMPHONY

William Henry Channing

To live content with small means; to seek elegance rather than luxury, and refinement rather than fashion; to be worthy, not respectable, and wealthy, not rich; to study hard, think quietly, talk gently, act frankly; to listen to stars and birds, to babes and sages, with open heart; to bear all cheerfully, do all bravely, await occasions, hurry never. In a word, to let the spiritual, unbidden and unconscious, grow up through the common. This is to be my symphony.

Quietly, frankly, without hurry: this seems so difficult in the city within the vise of deadlines and responsibilities. This summer, taking the time to just breathe more deeply and pluck at vegetables from the garden and watch a jumper dry on the clothesline and listen to the cicadas, and to heed the words of the *santonnier,* this summer, right now, has given me if not a symphony, at least a small and lovely song.

1 *August*

August begins. I feel for once curiously peaceful, as if I did not have to make any decisions at all or forever; to stay or to go; to anticipate or to remember; to act or remain passive. This is a moment of absolute, luxurious suspension. I like it.

Today we pray for the weather to hold through Dad's August 5 concert. We have been lucky with the sun, but, as Moth reminded us this morning, August typically deteriorates as the moon shifts and tugs at the approach of its next full belly and the big holiday, August 15, honoring the Assumption of the Virgin. We should expect a storm by then.

Our first visit here four years ago coincided with the break between July and August and, after two crisp days, the weather had indeed turned—neatly, precisely, dramatically—from cool dry July to steamy turgid August. And right on Moth's schedule we had endured one of the worst tempests to hit the valley. Rain came one afternoon and fell, was dumped really, and within an hour our front hall completely filled with water, gushing in from the downstairs loo. Grabbing whatever we could find to stem the cascade—buckets, ladles, sponges, towels—we bailed, and Bill dug a trench outside to divert the roiling waters. The next day, all had dried up and the only visible traces of deluge were wrinkles in the sandy soil, felled branches and crushed grasses in the fields, and the occasional teardrop on a leaf.

Today the *chaleur,* or heat, began to suffocate the house before ten, so we closed all the windows and curtains to hold in the cool. I have almost completed one pad of ink sketches and the Window Quilts as well, and I began a new series of collages using dusty, dusky images of highway given to me by a photographer I work with often. Roadworks: My own roads through the summer, an obvious project perhaps, but rather a mellow, wing-it exploit at this junction. For this group I want to select the shards and snippets in a trance, with my eyes squinted almost shut, to discover what turns up with each flick of the finger. The suspension of these last few days before departure, time held aloft on a spongy plateau or on a pillow, serves trance well. I work as if at a Ouija board. I have five photos to accept these scattered fragments of color and caption and window and wall and remnants of flower petal. Each Road separates and all Roads converge. I feel as if I will work fast on these—heart to head to hand—with no obstruction. I stretch and breathe into the vortex, and I hear Dad's slivers of melody slide under his door to mine, to interlock with my own song, melody to memory, sound to sight. We'll swim hard laps before lunch if we both continue at this pace.

2 August

Sarah is here. Her beloved and ancient Renault, the intrepid Eleanor which faithfully transported Sarah even as far as England and back, has emerged from the gloom of her garage in the village square and noses up to a mulberry near Peggy's Citroën. The shutters to Sarah's little one-room shed, where mules were stabled prior to the age of tractors, have been flung open and café-style iron chairs set out.

When Sarah reached university age, her mother gave her and her brother the mule shed and her brother remodeled it then, adding a sleeping loft and a cooking area and bath. In doing so, he uncovered "1751" chiseled into a roof beam, indicating that the shed and their mother's house as well undoubtedly predated the incision of these numerals.

At Sarah's behest, Jacques applied his horticultural skills to the terrace behind the shed, constructing an arbor upon which he trained vines to create a shady canopy for outdoor dining. I look forward to lunching with her there under the leafy pergola and glancing at the Lubéron from this different vantage from our own.

Two years ago we had talked through an entire day over wine and baguette sharing our love of land and art and times past and long gone, of people strolling in and out of our lives—people kind and heedless, callous and tolerant—in the sudden intimacy of

strangers turned friends through a bond of mutual though separate experience. For Sarah grew up even more entwined in the web of being a foreigner abroad, and since the age of six has straddled language and culture with an ease I cannot approximate. But I recall through her my own seven years of ferocious love of another place and I feel kin to her and to her spirit.

I realize that my Tuscany can never emulate her Provence. Sarah owns her own home here and thus enjoys a bond that can never be severed, whereas I disconnected my tie upon return to college and the States. If I recapture the essence of place this summer through identifying with this village, I ask her, am I only pretending to a claim? Because I reside here for only a month at a time and only every now and then, am I presumptuous to love this place so?

She thinks not. She offers me her shed as a roost any time I wish, and I am relieved to find in her a trust that can span longing with practical suggestion and with a promise. I had needed this summer as an interval of suspension—from my here-and-now family into my childhood family, and from my here-and-now work into my child-hood dream of artistic impulse—but I needed the summer, too, for something more than self, for some feeling that resonates to a sense of place and location.

I feel happiest, I realize talking with her, when balanced on a slender sill of tenuous dislocation, when straddling both the inside and the outside of a foreign place—and for me, as for her, a Mediterranean place—just as I did as a teenager. There will always be a part of me that will remain a foreigner back home, and, perhaps, there will always be a part of me that will remain foreign to my family as well. I needed this summer to allow that foreignness to resurface, without them, to explore this sensibility, this hunger, this desire, without imposing my need upon them. My family loved this place as a place to visit; I have loved this place as a place to live.

She and I could argue, and agree, that this valley should remain simple and undefiled, and as unpretentious as it was when Sarah was growing up here. We can argue, and agree, upon the magic of this valley, and our undiluted love for this village. But is it responsible of us, thinking to the future of the valley, to freeze it in our personal time and our personal need and is it responsible to feel it should not change, for its own sake?

This year Sarah's passion for the valley seems tempered by a more philosophical outlook. We have been persuaded, she too as much as I, that the impact of foreigners on this valley may be an invasion of sorts but that it also brings prosperity to many of her provençal friends, and to neighbors such as Jacques, who primps gardens throughout the valley, and the honeyman with his new boutique up in Gordes. A higher standard of living has evolved for many farmers

and shopkeepers through tourism. Because of foreigners and tourists, the deli in Coustellet is thriving, complete with new glassbrick walls and snappy awnings and exotic foods and drinks, and the *boulangerie* in Cabrières has relocated into fashionable new quarters doubled in size and volume.

If only the character of the littlest hamlets can hold, and that of the hill-villages too. Gordes casts a cynical eye on all visitors. And Roussillon is not the endearing hamlet Laurence Wylie wrote about thirty years ago in his *Village in the Vaucluse,* but just another tourist stop-by, with its cafés and off-street parking and postcard stands and ★ ★ ★'d restaurants—and robberies and, this summer, a rape. Will less-frequented villages such as Goult or Oppède succumb as well to the vagaries wrought by fame?

I told Sarah about going back to Florence longing to find it exactly as I had remembered it and about walking for hours through its skein of streets to touch my old house, about not finding it—and the panic, fearing I'd lost it, somehow, forever. But you found it? she asked. Finally: Yes. Was I longing for Florence, though? Or simply yearning for my own thin layer of innocent time within countless other layers of time, for myself in the company of the Brownings, say, or other travelers—foreigners, wanderers—skimming the casual, tolerant, forgiving surface of a beloved place, like dragonflies alighting upon a familiar and intimate pond?

This summer, padding barefoot around this place, I feel the same magic and an intensity matched only by the memory of a long-ago love. Maybe it is being a child to my parents again and maybe it is being separate from myself as a parent for a while. I have liked feeling both young and old, innocent and ancient, child and adult. I've liked listening to the fragments of language and understanding some but not everything of what I hear. I have loved being anonymous to some—yet known to others—as an American.

Sarah understands. She, too, finally returned to the States; she, as I, lives in America again. Neither of us wants to be an expatriate. Our roots are American. But we will always cherish nourishment from this Mediterranean sun.

3 August

A leaden and ominous day, a nonday or stay-in day: Dad's keyboard rhythms rat-tatted in desultory syncopations and my collages felt oozy under my fingers, as if the glue had a mind to wander.

Even Apollon stayed home.

But this density could soon explode into storm, which would be a good omen for the concert.

By evening the storm did break, as we hoped. At six, Béatrice had brought her boys by to shrug off their crankiness with a swim, and we stood at the fringes of the garden and pool and watched the glandular and swollen sky approach, bulldozing its grandiose grayness into the funnel of our valley.

Then rain. For the first time this summer we ate our supper indoors in Michael's tiny dining room under the stairwell. So refined with its collections of rare porcelains and tooled-leather, gilt-edged books and slim chandelier, the room does not coincide with our casual attire, but tonight it warmed us and made us feel snug and safe against the thunderclaps and ragged rippled rain.

4 August

During the night the rain increased and lightning darted back and forth from the Lubéron to Mont Ventoux; we relish this good water for all the plants and for the lawn. By morning the temperature had dropped so that we had to pull out blankets once again for the beds, and a mistral arrived, hard on the heels of the rain, puffing and tearing at the trees. Today the humidity dissolved. The air was cleansed again and clear.

We had to close all the doors, though, against the witchy wind, to restrain letter and collage bits from exploring the nether reaches of our rooms. Dad barricaded himself in his little "cabinet" to put the finishing touches on a song. I am beginning to wrap up collage work in any case, winding down to departure, allowing inspiration and motivation to drain off into little runnels like the rain. With just a couple of days to go, I start rooting and nudging, forcing snips and shards back into envelopes for packing, and I wrap finished collages in tissue to give to friends and officemates.

This summer, in its own guise as collage, or as journal: Following in the "booksteps" of authors I admire—a Henry James or an M. F. K. Fisher or an Elizabeth David or a Ford Madox Ford—creates an exercise in equations. What did he see? What do we see, Moth and Dad and I? What did she taste? What do we? What touches us? What nourishes us? What sensations of theirs seep under our skins and what of their sensibilities vibrates with our own?

With only three short visits here, I cannot pretend to ownership, as Sarah can, nor to an enduring association with this house, this village, this region, this land, except in memory, and, in fact, I could be, and perhaps should be considered a skimmer of sensations, relying as I do on the undersides of my feet and the topside of my tongue to communicate to me the grit and tang of this place. I do not know, nor do I remember, history or geography or politics or sociology except as an aside to what I see or hear or taste or touch or smell. I abandoned my academic self long ago; readings on these subjects yield an intellectual "ah-ha," and penetrate my gauzy brain with a zap of logic, a "so that's the story," but that's not what I needed or wanted or keep from this summer. I will remember little of that.

What I wanted and will take back with me is a sensuous connection, of skin to soil and sun and sky, as well as a kinship in feeling and focus with the artists and writers who cherished this region. I could not presume to their experience, but I share their love.

5 *August*

T . . . .
he invitation read:

> WE WOULD LIKE TO SHARE WITH YOU
> THE PLEASURE OF LISTENING
> TO FRANCIS THORNE
> —ON 5 AUGUST—
> INTERPRETING COLE PORTER.
> DINNER OUT OF DOORS WILL FOLLOW.

Even at a distance, from the road slaloming down into the valley
from the pinnacle of Gordes, we could pinpoint the dancing lights
fireflying around and about the hamlet-home where Dad was to
perform. Even at a distance, we sighted golden klieg-beams radiating
haloes into the trees surrounding the terrace where we were to dine.

Disembarking from the Souris, we dovetailed into the procession
of guests, some we knew, some we recognized, some we knew not
at all, trailing along the main graveled drive and cobbled pathway
past banks of uncut lavender aromatic with pregnant, unharvested
buds. Snatching at tendrils of chatter and greetings, and cheek-
kisses—left, right, left—we sensed that combination of excitement
and familiarity which promises a perfect party.

We have arrived just at that point in midsummer when holiday assumes its most comfortable rhythm, and the ease of routine flows into a mood of genial and complacent harmony and relaxation. At this point everyone has at last relinquished all homebound tensions, and the regearing for return in the autumn has not yet made itself felt. At this moment, everyone feels and is beautiful; everyone feels and is happy; everyone is ready for a song.

As we approached the dining terrace, set out with round tables scattered under the trees, the familiar scene—Lubéron, Gordes, and a swimming pool fluttering like a pale handkerchief—reflected the last streaks of sunset in exquisite relief.

Quite a crowd had assembled, a cosmopolitan bunch. Our Gordes hostess was there with her daughter, and we commented again on her lovely dinner and the deadly wasp, and Peggy sat close by. Dad's "theater" awaited him—the sliding glass doors pulled back into their wallpockets and piano poised with speakers to each side.

All morning Dad had practiced here, blending voice to keyboard, and now, on cue, the program began, with one melody slipping into the next, gathering gasps of delight, some murmured sing-alongs and tapping toes. Unlike the early-summer houseparty silence, a spirited hum surrounded Dad's songs. This moment too, when my summer was about to draw to a close, I felt carried aloft on song, my own hum happily in tempo, in tune, and, looking around, I saw everyone felt the same, whether or not they knew the words or the melodies or even the very Americanness of Dad's syncopations. It did not matter this time, and it felt good.

6 *August*

W...
hen I entered college I believed that I would become an art historian, and perhaps a Renaissance scholar, and probably an expatriate to boot. Skipping Art History 101, the Egypt-till-Today sweep, I settled into Medieval Architecture as an antipasto to future studies. Then, for sparkle and light—for contrast—I added Impressionism to my course load. The required tome was John Rewald's scholarly study of that period and its painters; on this lucent August evening we were invited by Rewald himself to visit his house, The Citadel, and to celebrate the arrival of the color proof of the cover for his most recent book, on the American collectors of works by his beloved Cézanne.

Fortunately for Rewald *et al.,* I swiftly abandoned art history as a goal and career. Adrift in detail and stunted into macaroni postures as a result of slouching in a dark auditorium staring at slides, I realized that I was not cut out to be an academic or a scholar of art. I could not drag minutiae from those slides which seemed to me disembodied specters of faraway, and far removed, masterworks. I could not touch them; I could not feel the ooze of the paint with my eyes. These shimmering transparencies were not close enough to the real thing for me; they seemed too distant to study properly, and somehow desiccated, deprived of their sinewy slurry paint.

So I transferred into Italian and into its mellifluous literature and filmscript as an antidote, hanging on to Dante and Pirandello and Moravia and Fellini in an attempt, I suppose now, to more audibly, more vocally, more volubly hang on to my faraway Florence.

Art, though, despite my abandoning its study, has always remained a love, and so I have looked forward to meeting Rewald.

Rewald's Citadel is just that: A rather menacing bulk, it hunches athwart a tapering butte, coming to a point, like a prow, to overlook the valley a hundred feet below. Access to the Citadel was through a sort of doggie-door set into an enormous studded gate. We bent almost double to enter, but straightening up inside, found ourselves in a long cool stone vault which opened, at its far end and through a wall of glass, to a pocket lawn shaded by a gigantic mulberry tree.

Our host, welcoming us with a chivalrous bow, urged us to tour around. With a wave of his hand he swept us up a series of lawn-carpeted steps to the prow where we could look back at the Citadel and down both sides of the sheer rockface to town and valley. A lone pine stood at the very point of the prow; two slighter pines supported a macramé-fringed hammock, a perfect escape for reading or napping, nearby. A comma of a pool, accentuated by narrow bands of cobalt tile, was spliced into a crook conveniently notched into the Citadel's northeastern wall—and just beyond us we could glimpse a tiny sheltered terrace centered by the kind of well one would toss a coin into for a wish.

Rewald had purchased the Citadel about the same time as Peggy and Michael formed their consortium in our village. A ruin then, all its stones had been violated by a slathered mantle of blistered concrete. All floors were dirt. A true fortress, the Citadel bore slit windows, trap doors, secret passages, and opportune holes for pouring hot oil that had once handily repulsed intruders. The ramparts still display a snaggle-toothed hemline, ragged and indomitable. Rewald pointed every hazard out to us in a voice both shaded by humor and vague threat, as if the joke on the guest would be to drop at his bidding into a subterranean abyss.

It took Rewald about a half-dozen years to make the Citadel habitable, peeling away the concrete to reveal the stones, tiling floors, adding doors. Each door, found during incessant flea-market prowls, is unique; each had required a custom-tailored aperture for a neat fit. One room is entered through a door from a confessional, another from a door from a nunnery, and so on. He gathered furniture, piece by piece, and also at flea markets, choosing styles compatible with the rigorously reconstructed and imposing interiors, mainly deeply carved, dark and grandly scaled furnishings that would not be intimidated by the rooms. Here and there on the walls he had hung sketches by some of his favorite Impressionists; appearing in these rooms somehow lighter than air, they add an unexpected fillip to the setting.

Conversation tonight centered on theater and music and art, and the cross-fertilization of language and culture, and, not unexpectedly, on the luxury of working and writing and thinking in a place such as this.

Looking over his color proofs, and commenting on his insistence on scholarly investigation, we ask if art these days has to be compromised for the sake of success? Can the artist express himself unequivocally and be accepted and acceptable both to an audience and to a marketplace? Just what is compromise?

What comprises art today? What constitutes music? What is theater—or dance or opera or architecture or writing? What art comes from the heart; how much is fueled by passion? And how much of what is called art is merely produced—to make money? What marks the fine line between self-expression and commodity?

My parents decry "junk" art, which they equate with the "junk bonds" flooding the marketplace. Because Dad promotes new, American classical music, he anguishes over the continuous struggle to get serious music performed—and funded. Music does not exist until and unless it is heard, and recorded. Only the most knowledgeable can "hear" music from a printed page. Competing against the amplified and engineered manipulations of contemporary popular music, which generates enormous profits for the recording companies, does serious music stand a chance to claim its own immortality?

Who is the audience?

Consider serious music as opposed to popular music, I remind them, in their own context: Dad and Moth lounge into '40s Big Band sound for their casual moments and I into '60s Golden Oldies. Whose preference is the more "authentic"? Is either experience less authentic than listening to a symphony? What would David, accustomed to reggae and rap, think?

Can we argue that it is simply better to have more people engaged in listening, in viewing, in touching and smelling and tasting the sensation of art, whatever that art may be? Is it preferable to listen to pop music than not to listen to any music at all?

Observing that 98 percent of all American households have a television set, one could argue that the very act of reading is dead. Yet thousands of books are published every year. But so few are read, someone says, and the only books that are read in any quantity at all are blockbusters or mysteries or horror stories. Why not wait for the movie or television miniseries?

Everyone in our group had read a best-seller this summer, on Picasso, measuring it against a picture book we've known for years which shows the artist posturing in front of an adoring camera. Which book is an accurate portrayal of this artist, or of an artist at all, or of art? Although I've always found Picasso's prodigious energy and his output awesome, and his influence on art and artists perfectly valid, I've never quite trusted his claim to genius. I have always shrunk from the anger in his eyes, from his overpowering ego, from his tormented and abusive vision of women.

His explosive and vulgar urgency, his careering back and forth between longing and love and anger and hate, his irreconcilable demons and his volatile moods were and are so sensational—and so conspicuously commercial. More than any other painter, perhaps, Picasso, to me, sums up the conflict between making art and marketing art, between making self and selling image.

I continue to imagine art as a gift first, or a benediction, and one that should be sustained throughout a career. I continue to believe in art as an act of communication, to be shared on faith, and not only through defiance.

Artists are egocentric, there is no doubt about it, and they always defy their audience on some level to believe as they do. They always test the reach of communication. I know I must acknowledge the selfishness in myself too. I know I must stretch my soul's resilience to coincidentally trust and defy, to equally antagonize and share, and to reconcile both love and anger in the same gesture of faith.

I look askance at Picasso, I realize, because I envy him his rage: It could be mine as well. And I recognize his longing for wholeness: It could be mine as well. The man pressed sharply and continuously against his edges, but he never quite made the leap beyond. Perhaps he, unlike van Gogh or Mozart, sensed more acutely the danger of madness outside his window—and felt he dared not risk that last consummate reach. His obsession could only go so far.

It seems that today more and more artists ride on the magic of identity, letting their persona, more than their art, communicate as the medium, as the message, the package, the marketable force. If this is the case, then, does genius matter; does madness?

7 *August, last Sunday*

Today is the day for "lasts": last drive–about, last errands, last glimpses of the valley, a last drink with friends, before departure. We attempted a small jaunt first into Gordes to purchase postcards for Moth, but there were so many automobiles pulled up into the photo–opportunity overlook and so many tourists backing up into the road to focus their cameras that we had to turn back. Instead we drove over, at my request, to L'Isle to inspect a new and quite grand antiques consortium reputed to display and sell the finest provençal antiques and collectibles in the area.

Eleven *antiquaires* collected their wares under the high trussed roof of L'Espace Bechard at the outskirts of town, in a cavernous barn of a gallery; their individual stalls march along a wide aisle, each composed like a still-life painting. The selection of objects, each object more exquisite than the next, was perfectly agreeable, perfectly juxtaposed, perfectly in harmony with the whole—and perfectly typical of Provence: huge squares of thick quilted provençal-print fabric; lushly fringed and weighty dark-toned paisley shawls; sinuous serpentine-backed three-seater painted settees with handwoven rush seats; round tilt-top walnut or cherrywood tables used for wine tastings; stately birdcages constructed like miniature châteaux; hand-painted eighteenth- and nineteenth-century faïences; white Marseilles bedspreads; monogrammed table linens; hatboxes. The prices escalate so during the summer season, we found no bargains; prices, indeed, virtually match or even surpass those in New York.

The utter refinement of each object, for once, made me wish to own everything! Usually I feel nothing of the kind; I find that transporting a "look" such as French Provincial back home often results in settings that seem pretentious and costumey. The provençal look is stylish and wildly popular in the States, I know, but best put into perspective, when combined with American things and allowed to breathe in an American ambience.

Less imposing, but no less typical than the antiques gallery, is a little museum we visited across the valley in Bonnieux—the Musée de la Boulangerie. A bakery museum. How very French, we thought, to devote a townhouse to a collection, just as graciously presented as the Espace Bechard's antiques—but of baking tools, breads of all shapes, historic ephemera such as tax receipts—plus, rather bizarrely, a cache of pinioned insects under glass? On the ground level, the museum re-creates an authentic provençal kitchen in one room, complete with all the specific furnishings, such as the *panetière,* associated with making and storing bread. And at the entrance stands a George Segal–like plaster baker hefting his loaves into an enormous bread oven.

One of the greatest pleasures of this summer has been the fresh bread and the daily routine of going out each morning to purchase our croissants and baguettes warm from the oven, exchanging greetings and weather-chat. To cherish bread, coaxing shapes both simple and fanciful from the elastic and forgiving dough, sculpting and caressing flour, egg, and shortening into loaf or crescent, seems the perfect symbol of life here: making the staff of life, this stuff of life, into something more—into a work of art.

Or, simply, the work itself is art. In bread, sense and sensation coalesce: taste and touch, smell and sight, and even an audible sigh. The eyes knead, the ears taste, the tongue listens.

And to combine bread with wine, as we do every evening at dinner, emulating the young priest's act of communion with loaf and flask,

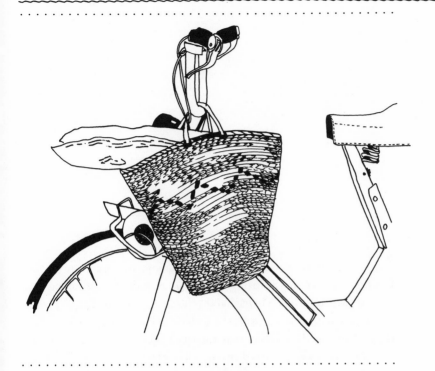

brings into accord the earthy with the spiritual, the mundane with the sublime, the everyday with the divine. No wonder the little *santons* were once sculpted from bread!

For me this summer had offered in sympathetic abundance this symmetry of sensibilities. The same harmony I experience in breaking bread and sipping wine has resonated in collage-making or drawing or reading, internal activities I have enjoyed in the quiet of our village. Perhaps, in a way, our village has felt too quiet this summer because of the illness of its patriarch, and I've missed the sense of shared activity we knew four years ago, and especially of a Sunday when everyone gathered in the square to play *boules;* but, in a way, our respectful silence and mutual vigil serves to honor another sense of community, another symmetry—the reality of ongoing life with the reality of eventual death.

Last day

Early morning was consumed by cleaning, to prepare my room for houseguests do-si-doeing with me as I depart. Washing and drying the sheets *à la* Michael and replacing everything in the room as it was when I arrived proved a welcome distraction and lent a lazy rhythm to this day. Back went the rug under the beds covering up the gritty tiles that caressed my feet to unyielding callus. The card-table folded its legs under it like the spider in the loo and was tucked neatly back into the upstairs closet next to Moth and Dad's suitcases, and the armoire and *semainier* were purged of my miscellaneous possessions. Books stack back upon the nighttables and new flowers bloom upon the dressing table. Bedspreads rest again upon the freshly made beds. A quick scan for scorpions reveals no lurking trespassers. Wasps hustled back out to their roof tiles were inhibited from reentry by screens secured once again with a new mesh of Nicollet Island thread.

But then: time. This waiting-room feeling before departure is always sad and disconcerting. I want to leave and I want to stay. Moth suggested I accompany her in a quick circular swing down to Coustellet's deli and on over to Cabrières, to gather today's bread, a double-order to welcome their incoming guests. And then, a snack, load my suitcase into the Souris, and so to Avignon and away.

188

Out: Under our archway, almost nudging Philippe's Renault. Into the *place* where Sarah's Eleanor and the Citroën shimmer in the heat and the postman deposits envelopes in the metal boxes clustered on Jacques's wall. Turn left: Past the honeyman's goose pen and the *chambre d'hôte* and *poubelles* ranked in a row. Onto Apollon's road and the dirt track swinging over the gorse to Béatrice's house. Off to the northwest, the diorama of Jean and Chouchou's hamlet shrinks behind the scrim of noonday haze, and, beyond, at the fork to the access to the N100, a soggy pool that appeared in July has spread its malignant ooze. It has killed two cherry trees at the roots.

And then: Inevitable flight. The thrust and tug of the N100 and the D2 pull us out of the valley, leaving it behind, to its own August.

I shall miss the long loose tango of days, hugging routine and letting it go, as I please. I'll miss the scent of rosemary growing wild by the wall next to the laundry line and the flash of butterflies when Philippe hoses the lawn. I'll miss the crunch of sun-dried jumper against my back and the sting of vagrant gravel between my toes. I'll miss the wrinkled skins of oil-burnished olives washed down with the Système U's astringent rosé.

Driving, we talk of houses past and other summers. Of a house on the Mediterranean Sea we summered in, when I was twelve, swollen with Brahms and bulldogs. Of a house on a marsh in South Carolina redolent of sulphur and low tide. And a house in Bermuda syncopated with calypso and playing cards. I almost hesitate to reflect on this month. By doing so I may victimize it; will I drown it in nostalgia and yearning as I once did Florence and those other child-places in my heart? Places I only own in memory.

Not owning, not owning this place, except for a few weeks—to what and to how much am I entitled? Does cherishing this place become something of an obscene act, something quick and easy, rather than enduring? What is rootedness, anyway? Can the illusion of ownership be as truthful or as sustaining as the real thing?

I've never owned a place that connected me so. Our apartment nine floors up back in New York always feels airborne, in flight, somehow transitional, even after fifteen years.

Here I have felt at ease away from my real home but at Real Home, loving our Simple Life and the Mediterranean sun. Here I have felt at ease in a multitude of simultaneous guises: woman and child, adult and daughter, artist-of-sorts and art lover, traveler and tourist. Being a foreigner in this foreign place permitted a weaving back and forth between heritage—who I was or am—and possibility—who I am or could be. Within the comforting hug of my childhood family, I could revert to testing the boundaries of my own safety and I now look forward to the boundaries of my family back home. Being here, I admitted to myself the part of me that has never grown up or perhaps refuses to and never will. It felt good to expose the part that needed to touch the past.

I needed this past, this sojourn, I suppose, quite simply to proceed with my present and with whatever is to come. I am not sure I will ever resolve my dilemma. I have a recurrent dream, of running through an airport and never quite making the plane. My destination, I suppose, is: where?

80/86

FOR THE BEST IN PAPERBACKS, LOOK FOR THE

In every corner of the world, on every subject under the sun, Penguin represents quality and variety—the very best in publishing today.

For complete information about books available from Penguin—including Pelicans, Puffins, Peregrines, and Penguin Classics—and how to order them, write to us at the appropriate address below. Please note that for copyright reasons the selection of books varies from country to country.

In the United Kingdom: For a complete list of books available from Penguin in the U.K., please write to *Dept E.P., Penguin Books Ltd, Harmondsworth, Middlesex, UB7 0DA.*

In the United States: For a complete list of books available from Penguin in the U.S., please write to *Dept BA, Penguin*, Box 120, Bergenfield, New Jersey 07621-0120.

In Canada: For a complete list of books available from Penguin in Canada, please write to *Penguin Books Ltd, 2801 John Street, Markham, Ontario L3R 1B4.*

In Australia: For a complete list of books available from Penguin in Australia, please write to the *Marketing Department, Penguin Books Ltd, P.O. Box 257, Ringwood, Victoria 3134.*

In New Zealand: For a complete list of books available from Penguin in New Zealand, please write to the *Marketing Department, Penguin Books (NZ) Ltd, Private Bag, Takapuna, Auckland 9.*

In India: For a complete list of books available from Penguin, please write to *Penguin Overseas Ltd, 706 Eros Apartments, 56 Nehru Place, New Delhi, 110019.*

In Holland: For a complete list of books available from Penguin in Holland, please write to *Penguin Books Nederland B.V., Postbus 195, NL-1380AD Weesp, Netherlands.*

In Germany: For a complete list of books available from Penguin, please write to *Penguin Books Ltd, Friedrichstrasse 10-12, D-6000 Frankfurt Main 1, Federal Republic of Germany.*

In Spain: For a complete list of books available from Penguin in Spain, please write to *Longman, Penguin España, Calle San Nicolas 15, E-28013 Madrid, Spain.*

In Japan: For a complete list of books available from Penguin in Japan, please write to *Longman Penguin Japan Co Ltd, Yamaguchi Building, 2-12-9 Kanda Jimbocho, Chiyoda-Ku, Tokyo 101, Japan.*